art workshop
PASTELS

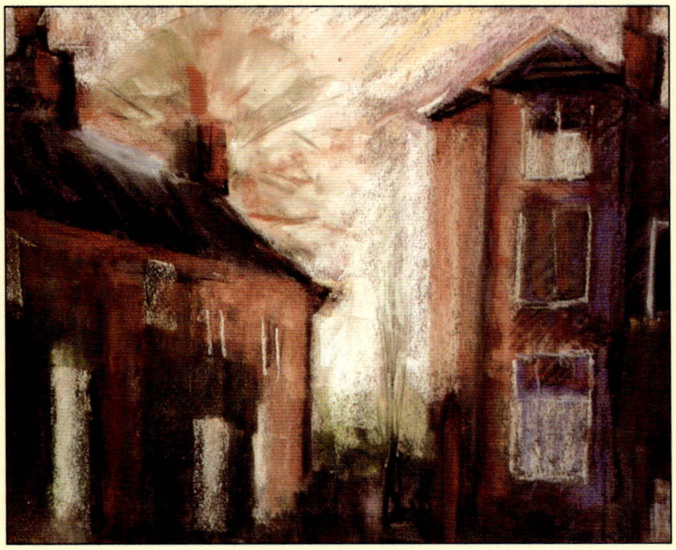

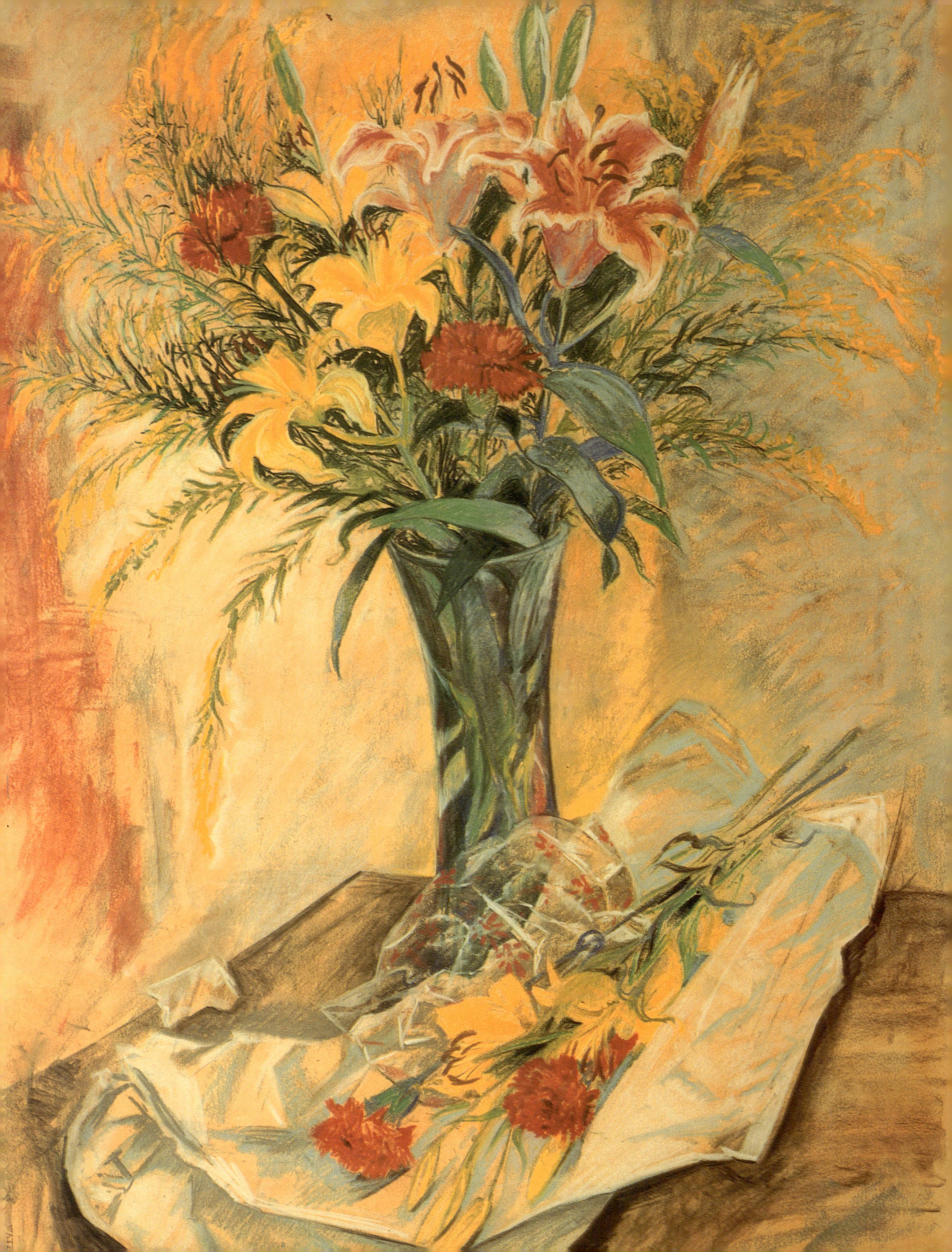

art workshop
PASTELS

STEP-BY-STEP TEACHING THROUGH INSPIRATIONAL PROJECTS

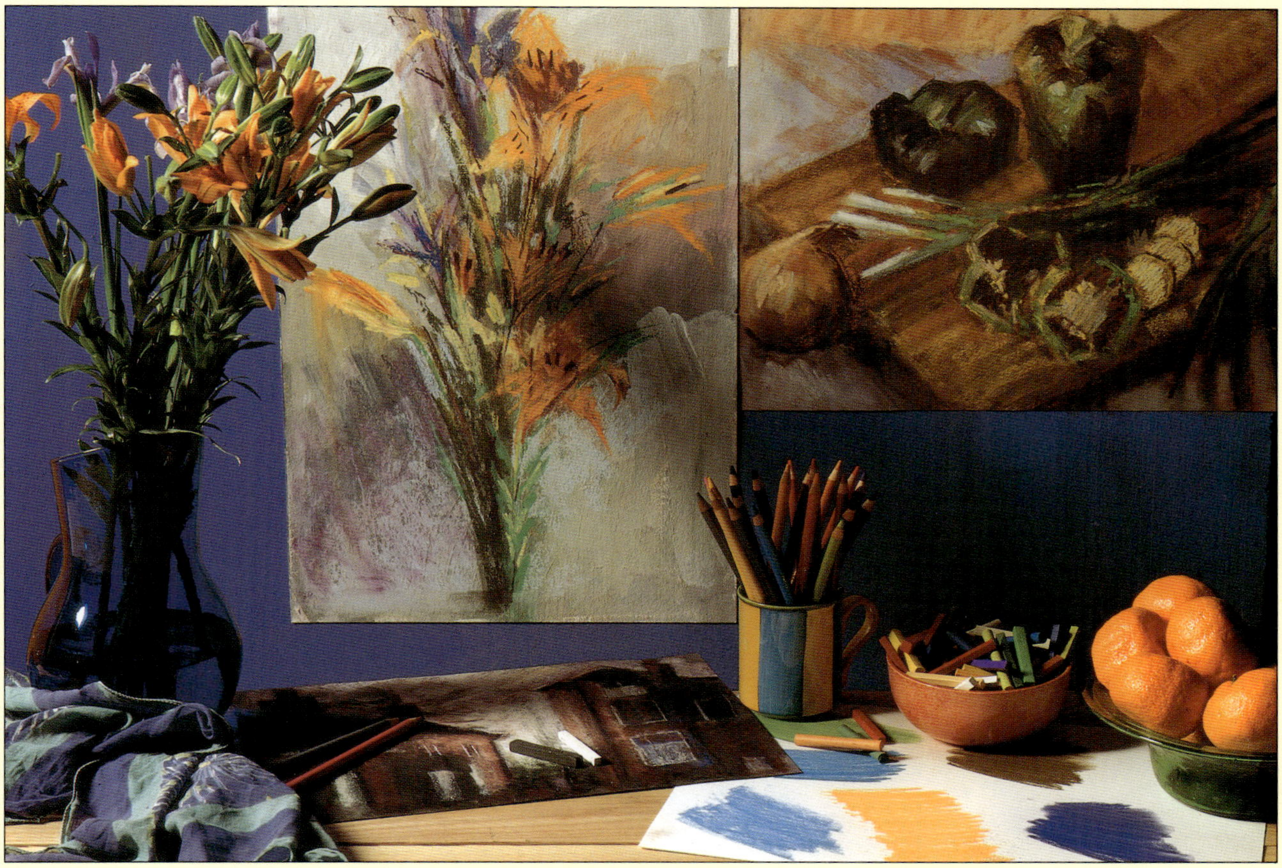

hazel **harrison**

HH
HERMES
HOUSE

Paperback edition published by Hermes House
an imprint of
Anness Publishing Limited
Hermes House
88-89 Blackfriars Road
London SE1 8HA

All rights reserved. No part of this publication may be reproduced, stored in a retrieval system, or transmitted in any way or by any means, electronic, mechanical, photocopying, recording or otherwise, without the prior written permission of the copyright holder.

A CIP catalogue record for this book is available from the British Library

ISBN 1 84309 518 1

Publisher: Joanna Lorenz
Project Editor: Samantha Gray
Designer : Michael Morey
Photographers :Paul Forrester and John Freeman

Printed and bound in Singapore

© Anness Publishing Limited 1996

1 3 5 7 9 10 8 6 4 2

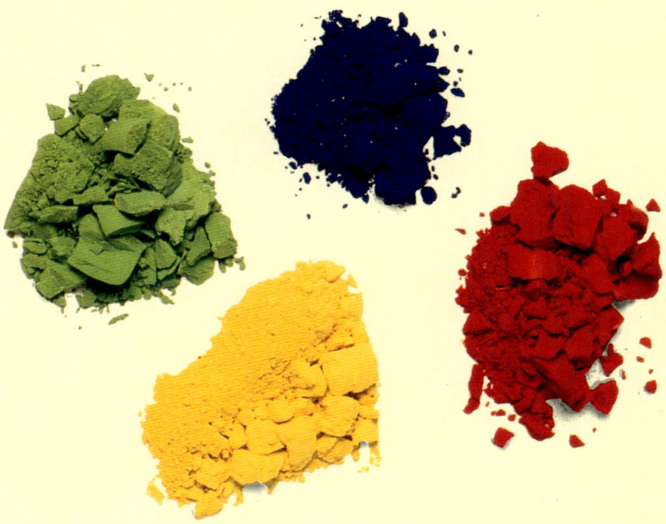

CONTENTS

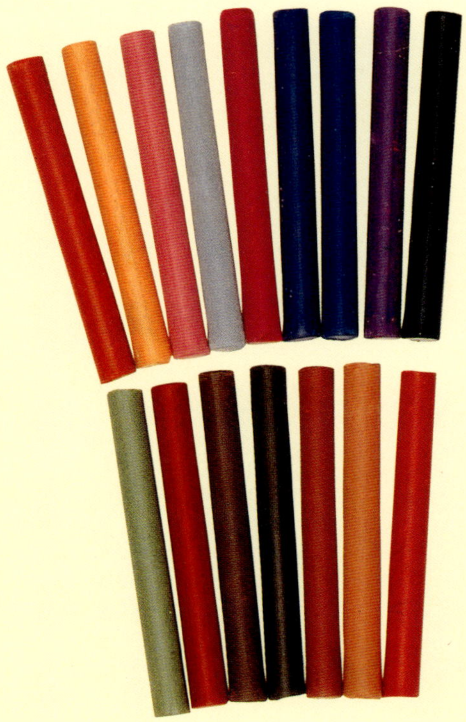

Introduction

ABOUT PASTELS

Pastel is unique in that it is both a drawing and a painting medium. It tends to be associated with drawing because the colours are not applied with a brush, but the medium's malleability and richness of colour invite a painterly approach. Many of today's artists exploit this effect in pastel to produce works which at first sight look almost like oil paintings.

Pastel is rapidly becoming one of the most favoured painting media, vying with watercolour for popularity. One of the reasons for this is probably that pastel sticks simply look so beautiful – open one of the boxed sets of pastels in an art shop and you will see a rich array of colours, which seem to offer a direct invitation to the artist. A tube of paint is a poor thing by comparison because you can't see the colour until you have squeezed it out.

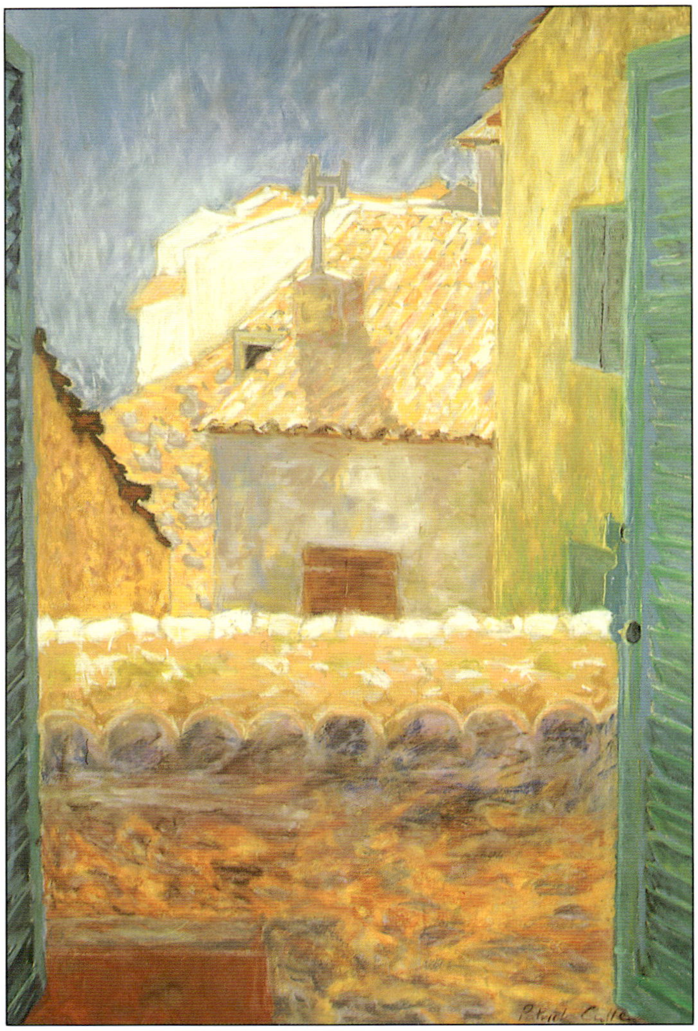

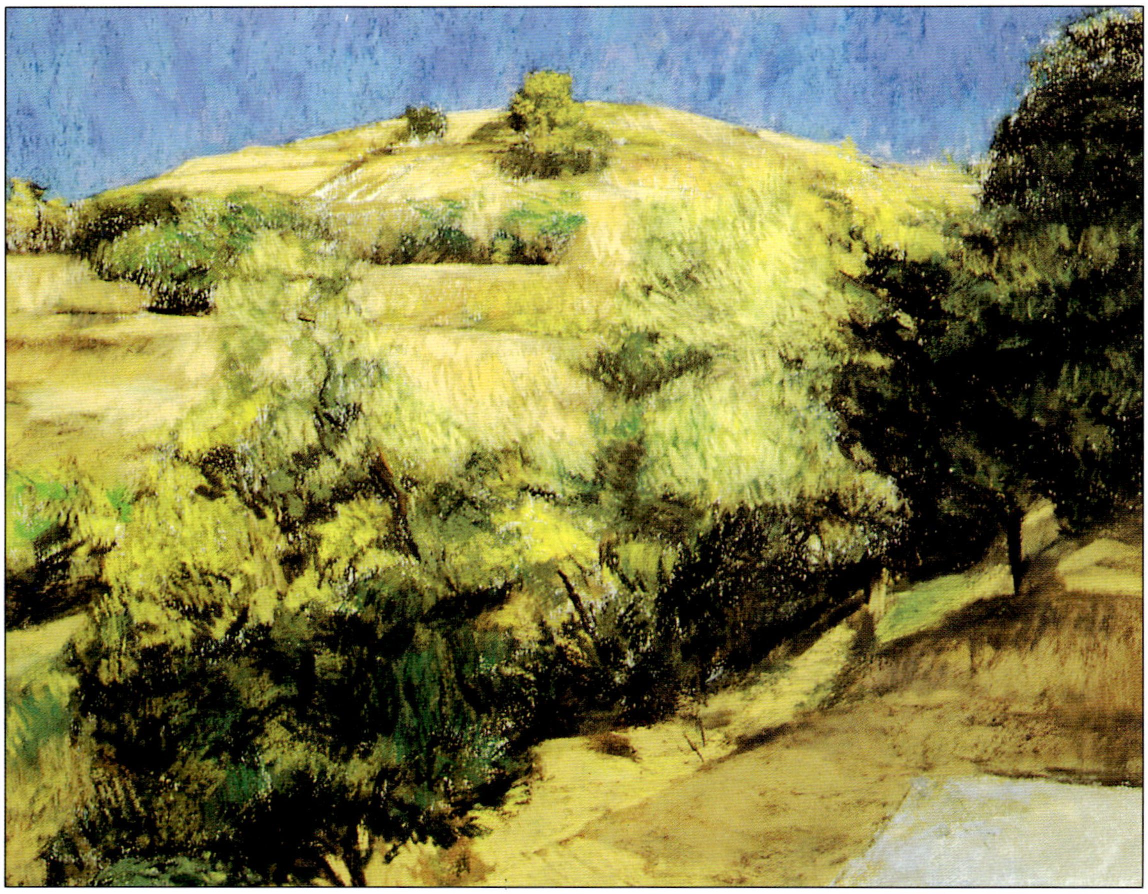

JAMES CRITTENDEN
SUMMER HILLSIDE
(Left) *Pastel is often associated with delicate colours, hence the term "pastel shades", but this powerful landscape shows that considerable depth of tone can be achieved by laying one colour over another. The artist has given a lovely feeling of life and energy by the way he has used the pastel strokes; in the trees, particularly, the effect is very much like brushstrokes in an oil or acrylic painting.*

PATRICK CULLEN
WINDOW IN PROVENCE
(Opposite) *The colours are also built up thickly in this painting, but the technique is very different, with short pieces of pastel used to make broader marks. To create the gentle but luminous colours, the artist has restricted himself to light and mid-tones, controlling them carefully, and changing the direction of the strokes to give variety to the different surfaces.*

KEN PAINE
HEAD OF A YOUNG WOMAN
(Right) *This artist exploits the directness and expressive qualities of pastel in his portraits. He works with great rapidity, usually beginning by building up the tonal structure with a monochrome "underpainting" made with broad strokes of short lengths of pastel. Linear definition and bright colour accents are left until the final stages. The coloured paper is still visible in areas.*

MAUREEN JORDAN
ROSE AND GERANIUM TEXTURES
(Below) *The artist has exploited the whole range of pastel techniques in this vivid and lively picture, combining solid, thickly applied colour, blended in places, with fine-line drawing to pick out individual flowers and petals. In the foreground, an area which can become dull in a floral group, a series of strong, decisive marks creates its own pattern and interest.*

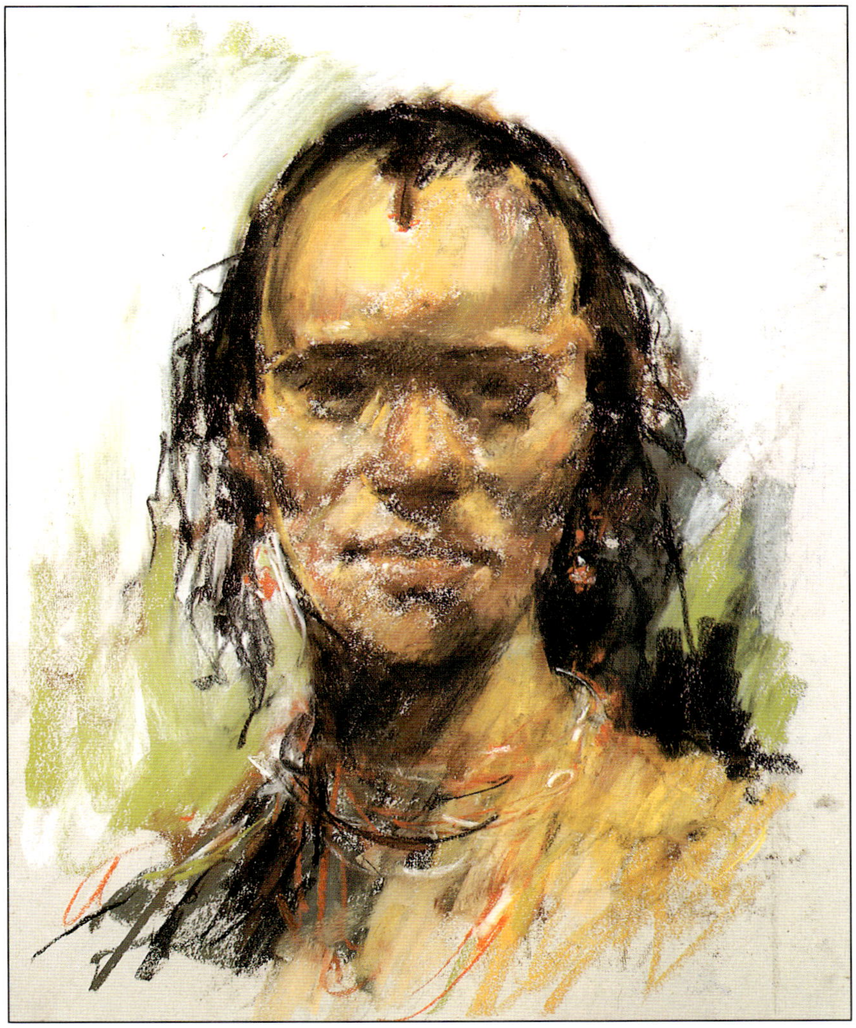

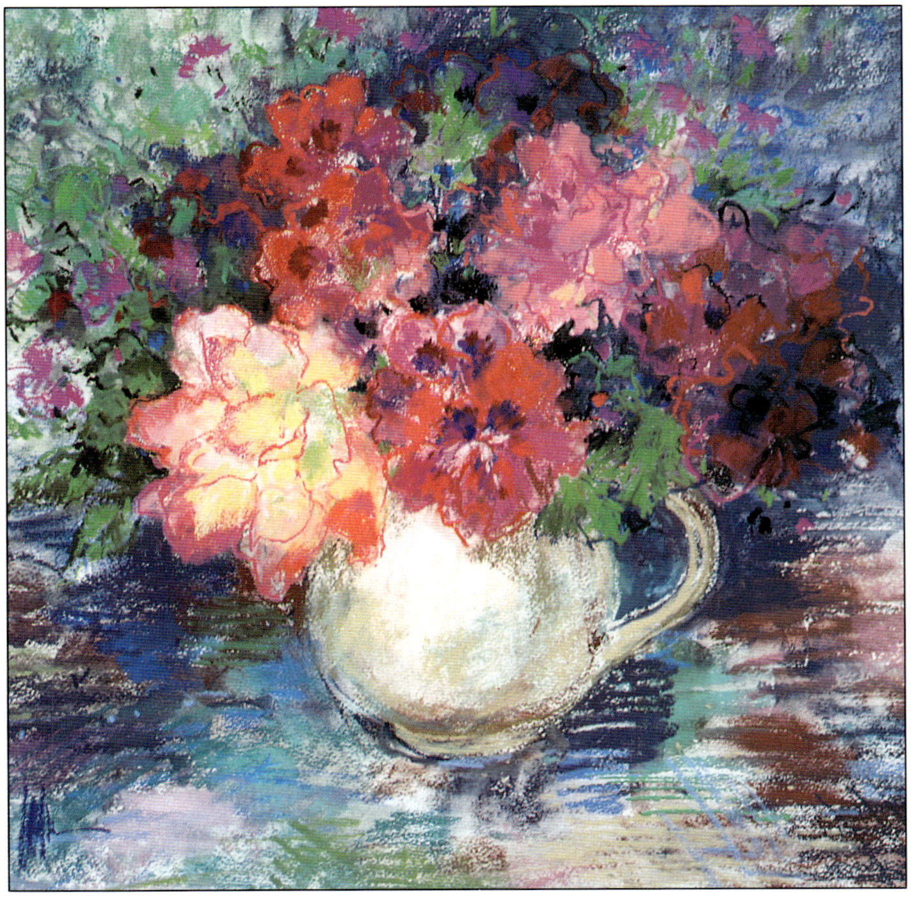

PROS AND CONS

The immediacy of pastel is also appealing. These sticks of colour form a direct link between your hand and the paper. You don't have to mix colours on a palette and you need no brushes. Like any drawing medium, pastels are responsive, easy to manipulate and quick to use, which makes them ideal for outdoor work and rapid effects; but because of their loose, crumbly texture and brilliance of colour – pastels are almost pure pigment – they can also be built up thickly in layers just as paints can. As you will see from the small gallery of paintings shown here, pastels are a versatile medium and there are many different ways of using them.

No medium is perfect, however, and those who are not accustomed to pastels may experience some problems until they become familiar with techniques involved, and learn what pastels can and cannot do.

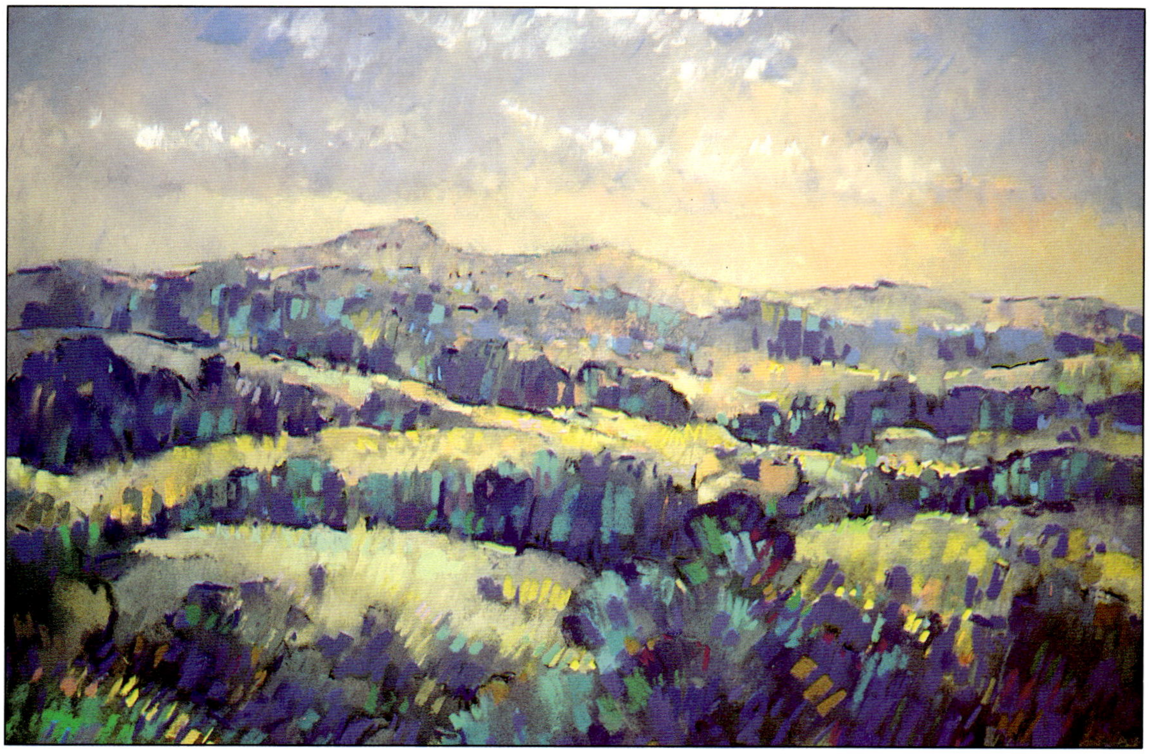

GEOFF MARSTERS
LANDSCAPE IN THE AUVERGNE
(Left) *When he first took up pastels, Marsters was determined to use the medium as a painting rather than a drawing technique, and through constant experiment he has evolved his own methods of working. He achieves his rich, dense colours by working on abrasive (pumice) paper, rubbing the pastel into it, fixing and then applying further layers on top. He loves the brilliance of pastels, and exploits this quality by "keying up" the colours.*

One of the advantages of pastels – that you do not have to pre-mix colours – can also work against you. Any mixing has to be done on the working surface but, because it is not possible to try out mixes in advance as you can with paints, it is all too easy to make mistakes. You cannot erase pastels easily, although you can correct mistakes to some extent by laying more colours on top. If you do too much of this, however, you will clog the paper surface and may end up with a tired-looking, muddy painting.

One of the greatest exponents of pastel, the 18th-century portrait painter Maurice Quentin de La Tour, mentioned the possibility of spoiling work by over-mixing; he had one or two other complaints, too – about the dust generated by working with pastels, for example. It has to be admitted that it is not a medium for those who like to keep their floors clean. It is hard on the hands too, as they become covered with colour as soon as you pick up a stick.

A more serious problem is the fragility of pastels, in particular soft pastels. The sticks break very easily under pressure, added to which it is very easy to smudge finished work. Even when sprayed with fixative, the pigments tend to fall off the paper, especially if they rub up against another surface. Unless you can frame and glaze your work immediately, it is vital to store it carefully, laying it flat with pieces of tissue paper on top.

Despite these minor problems, pastel is a wonderful medium to use. Few who have taken it up, whether amateur or professional, feel inclined to abandon it.

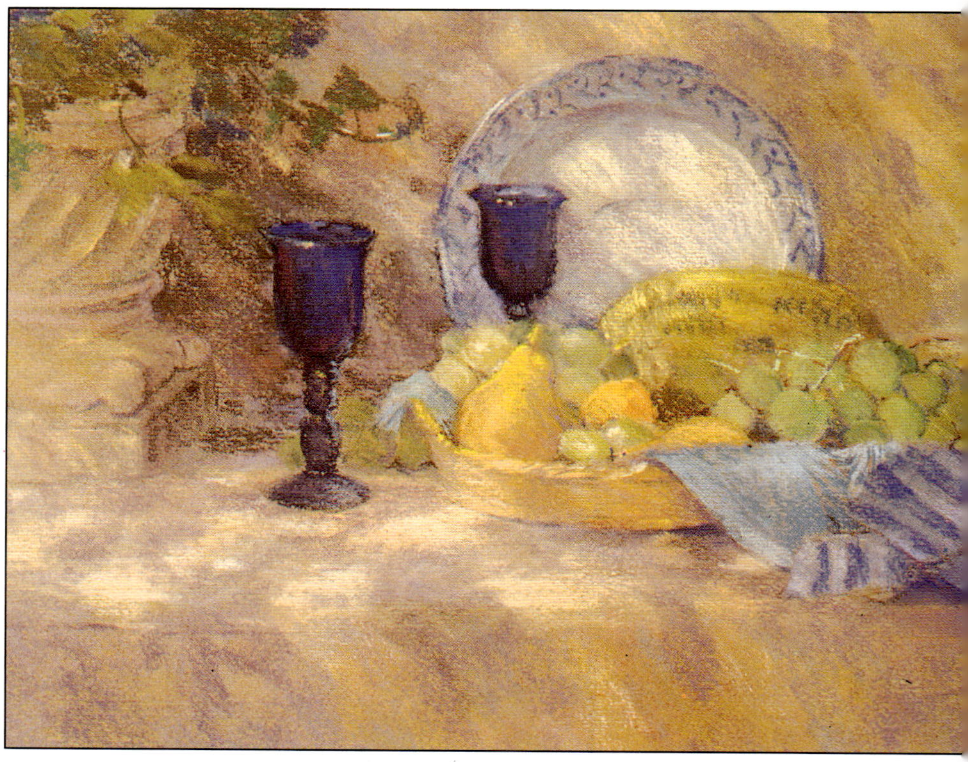

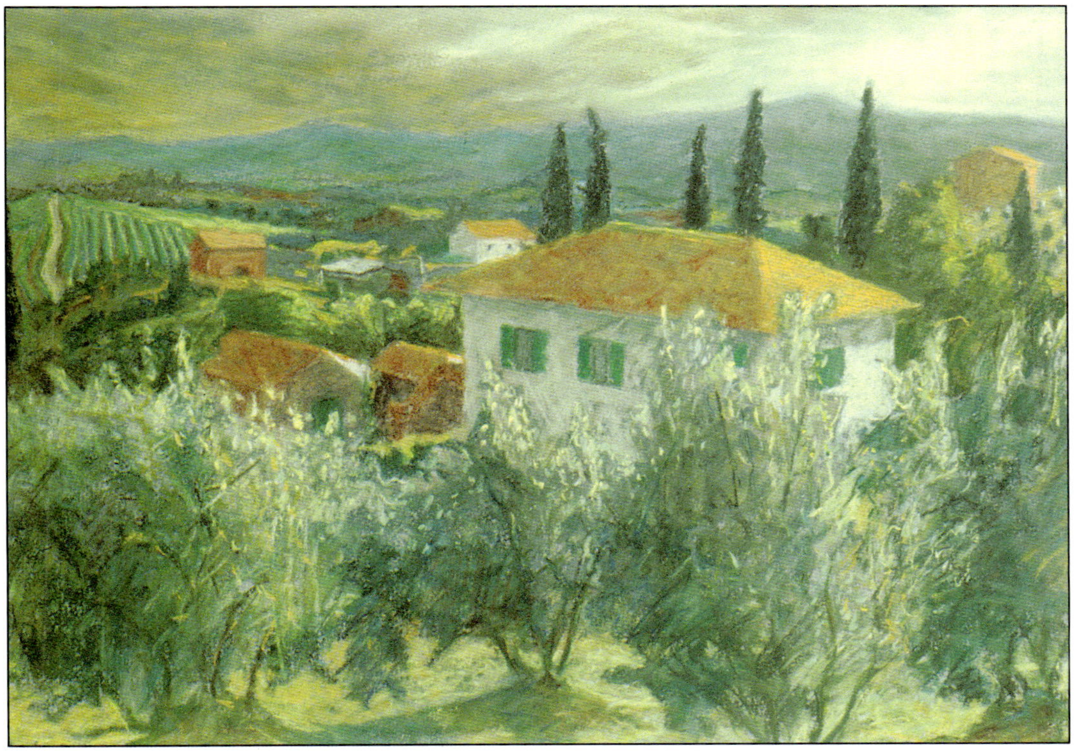

PATRICK CULLEN
CASA DE LIDO
(Left) *In this atmospheric painting, the approach to colour is more naturalistic than in the landscape opposite, but there are some similarities in technique, with the pastel again applied thickly and layered in places. Cullen usually works either on sandpaper, or on heavy watercolour paper on which he first lays a ground of watercolour.*

GEOFF MARSTERS
INTERIOR OF BOATHOUSE
(Right) *This subject, with its angularity and profusion of detail, might not seem suitable for a soft, crumbly medium such as pastel, which is usually considered better for broad effects, but the artist has treated it with great assurance. If you look closely you can see that the lines and edges are in fact quite loose and free; the impression of sharp linearity is created by the strong contrasts of tone and colour.*

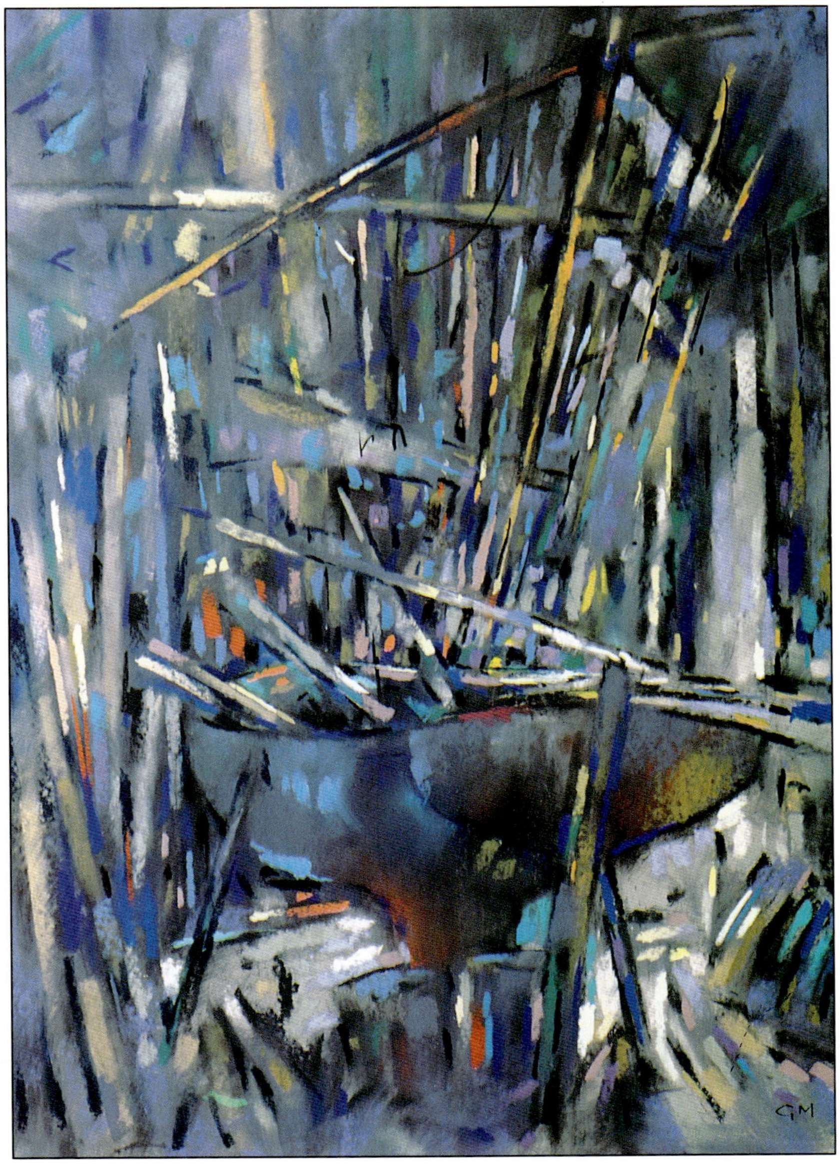

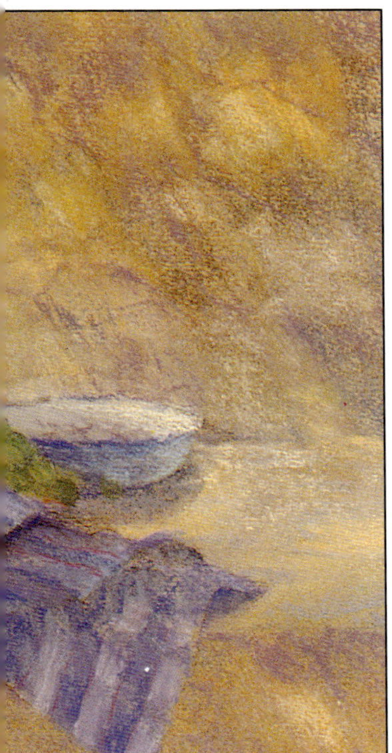

JACKIE SIMMONDS
STILL LIFE WITH BLUE SPANISH GLASS
(Left) *In this gentle and tranquil painting the artist has made clever use of pastel's capacity for creating a variety of textures. For the glass, deep blues have been blended to imitate the smoothness of the material, but the central area of the plate has been left slightly rough, while in the background several colours have been dragged lightly over one another.*

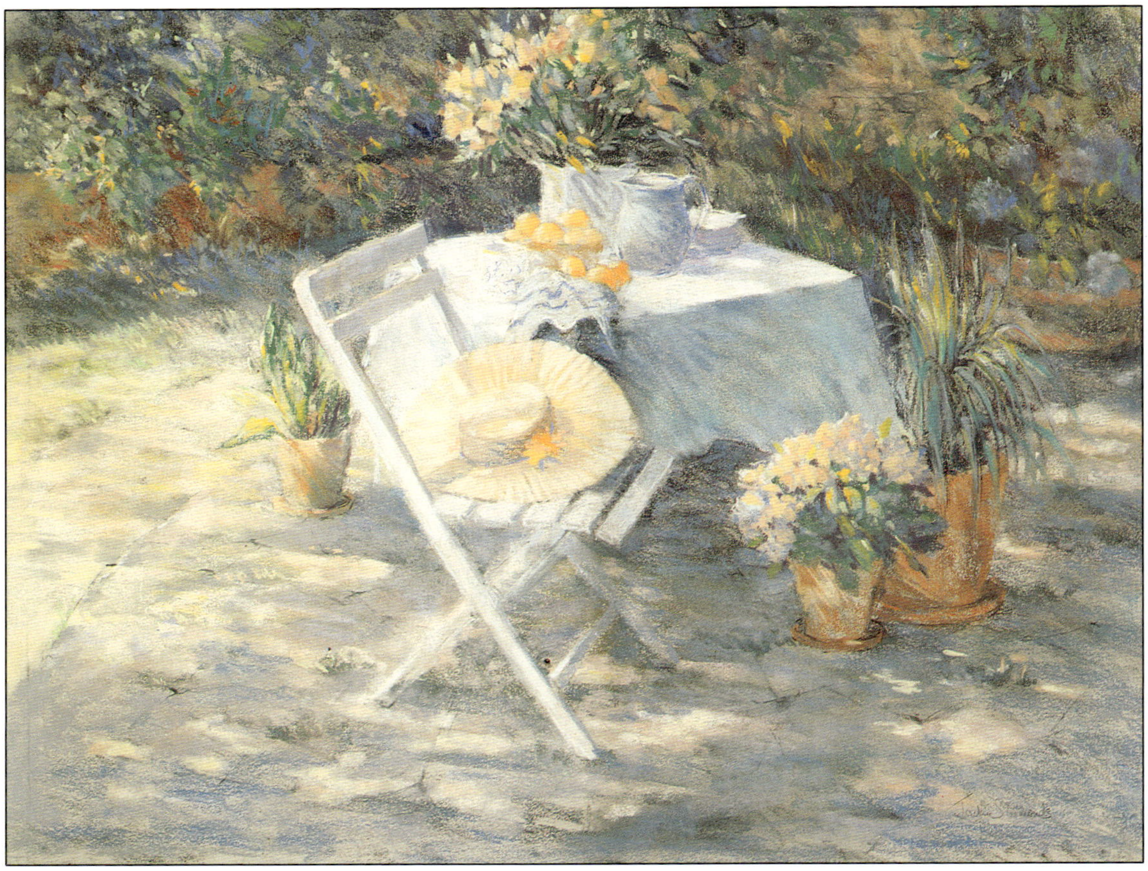

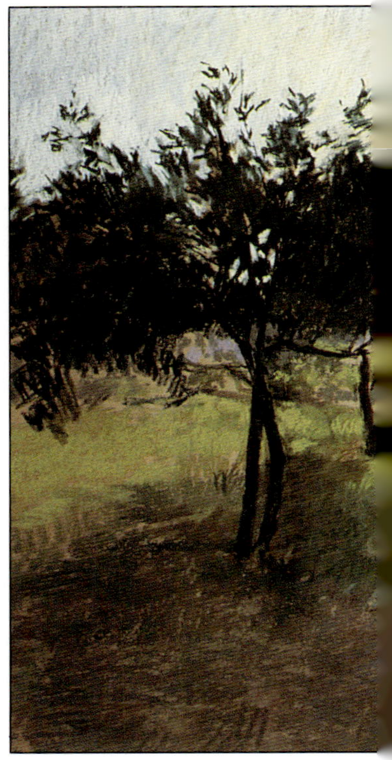

JACKIE SIMMONDS
TEA ON THE PATIO
(Above) *This delightful painting probably comes closest to most people's idea of pastel – the colours are light and fresh, in keeping with the airy subject, and the handling is delicate. In fact, however, these qualities owe more to the artist's skill in controlling the medium than to its inherent properties; it needs a light touch and a sound knowledge of both colour and technique to achieve such effects.*

ELIZABETH MOORE
STILL LIFE WITH PEARS AND PLUMS
(Below) *For this still life, the artist has worked in oil pastel, which she likes because it is related to oil paint, the medium she uses most frequently. She also finds it more controllable than soft pastel. Here it has allowed her to build up deep, rich colours as well as very subtle effects, notably the bloom on the plums.*

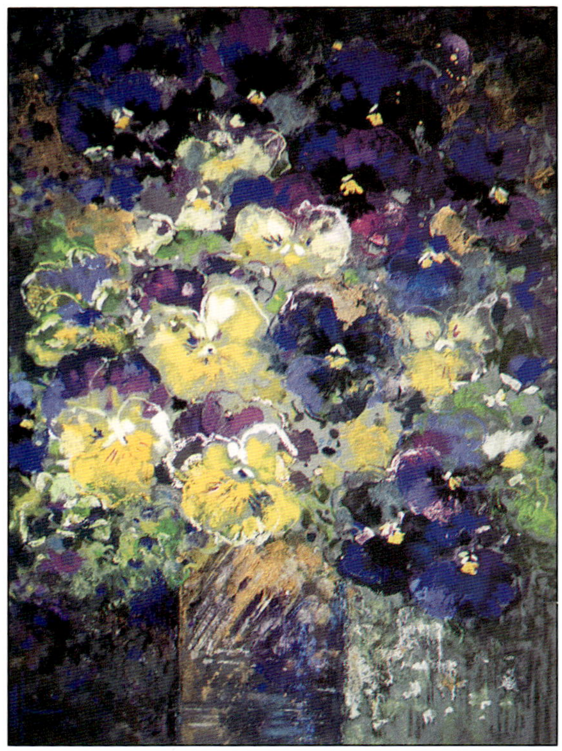

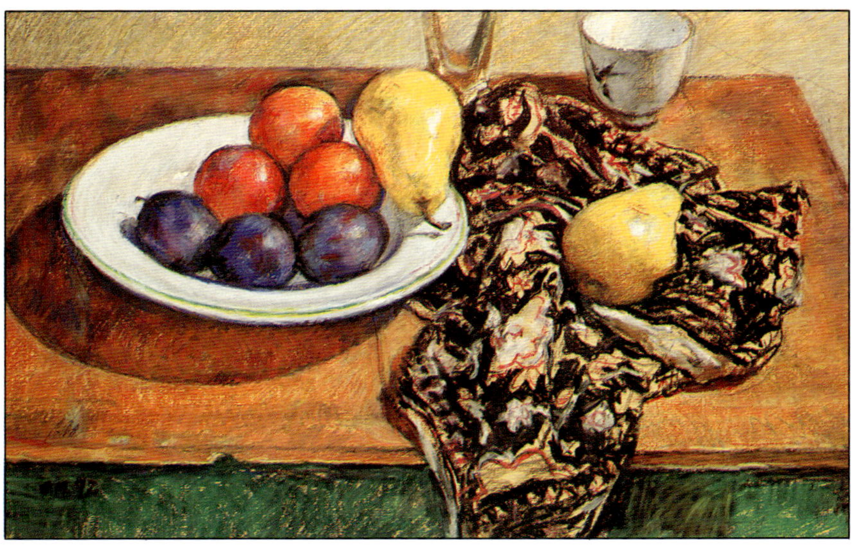

MAUREEN JORDAN
PANSY TEXTURES
(Above) *The characteristic crumbly texture of pastel can benefit from contrast with a smoother medium, and here the artist has used pastel in combination with acrylic. The acrylic underpainting has also allowed her to establish deep, rich colours from the outset without a heavy build-up of pastel.*

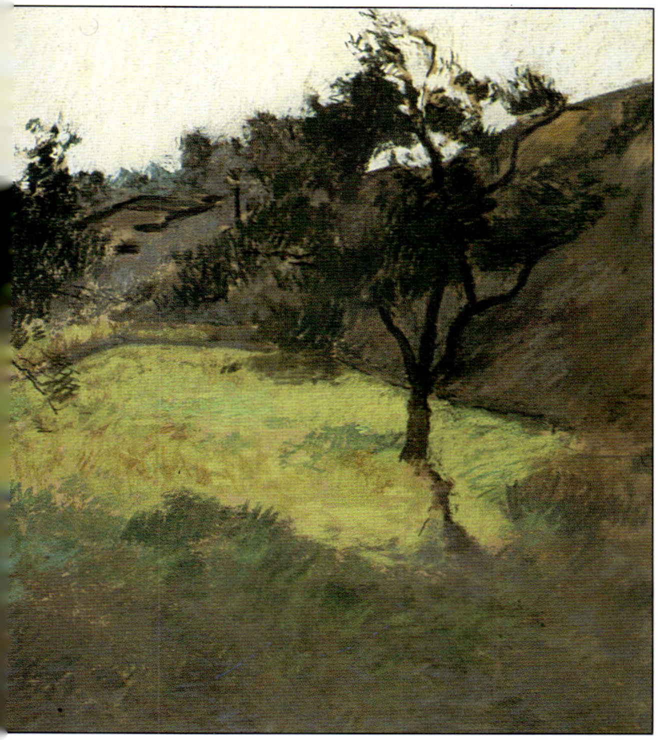

JAMES CRITTENDEN

ORANGE GROVE IN THE EVENING

(Left) *As in most of his pastel paintings, this artist skilfully combines the drawing and painting qualities of pastel to produce an interpretation of the landscape that is both realistic and highly personal. What appear at first glance to be solid areas of colour – the sky and grass – are in fact a complex network of overlaid lines and marks made with the tip of the stick, while the leaves of the trees are expressed by rapid calligraphic dashes and squiggles.*

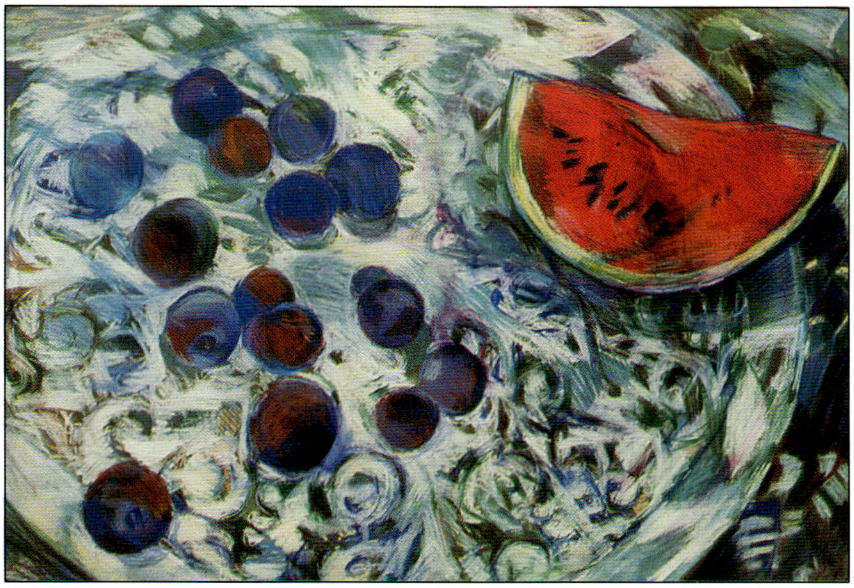

PIP CARPENTER

THE SUN-DAPPLED TABLE

(Right) *This painting, worked on a dark, greenish paper, gives the initial impression of oil pastel, but in fact is soft pastel pressed hard into the paper and fixed between stages to allow one colour to be laid over another. The artist was particularly excited by the effect of the light on the different surfaces – the volume of the fruit and the flat plane of the ornamental iron table.*

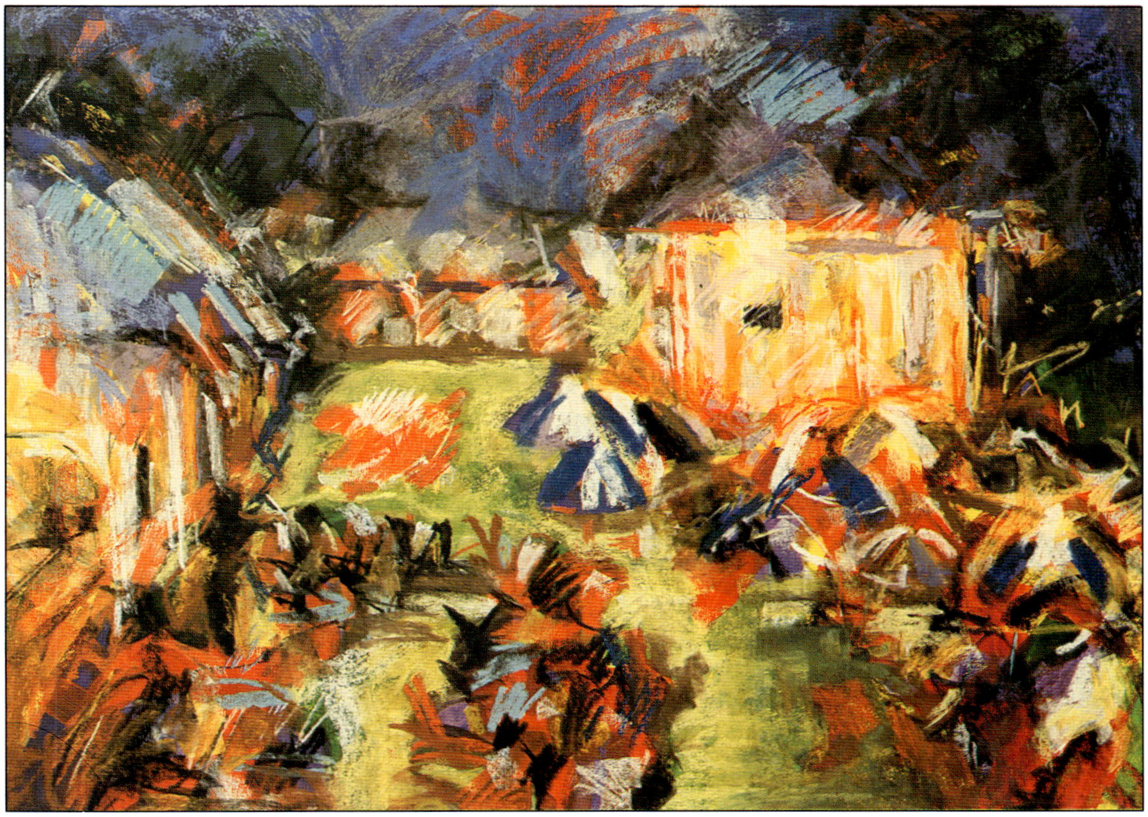

JUDY MARTIN

BANDSTAND SERIES

(Left) *Vivid colour was of primary importance in this painting, and here, too, acrylic has been used in combination with pastel. The underpainting, which set the colour-key for the picture, was mainly in shades of red and yellow, with contrasting colours of pastel applied on top in vigorous strokes. You can see this effect clearly in the sky, where strokes of blue pastel overlay bright red paint.*

PASTELS

There are four main types of pastel: soft (also known as chalk pastels), hard pastels, pastel pencils and oil pastels. All pastels are made in the same way. Ground pigment is bulked out with a "filler" such as chalk and held together with some sort of binder, the traditional one being gum tragacanth.

SOFT PASTELS

Very little binder is used in the manufacture of soft pastels, which are almost pure pigment, hence their brilliance of colour, fragility and powdery texture. Although the majority of pastel painters use soft pastels, you may find hard pastels and pastel pencils form a useful complement to these.

HARD PASTELS

Hard pastels contain more binder and have a finer consistency. They do not break so easily and can be sharpened to a fine point for detailed work. Some artists use the side of a hard pastel stick to block in large areas of colour in the preliminary stages of a painting. Because they are less crumbly than soft pastels, they are easier to work over with other colours as the work progresses. They can also be used on their own, but in general they are better suited to pastel drawing, where the approach is more linear, than to pastel painting. The range of colours is also quite limited, at least in comparison with soft pastels, where the colour variations are truly awesome.

PASTEL PENCILS

These are also more of a drawing than a painting tool, but a few pastel pencils will form a useful addition to your kit; they are ideal for small areas of detail in a painting as well as for making preliminary drawings. Ordinary graphite pencils should never be used for underdrawings for pastel, as graphite is slightly greasy and will repel any pastel colour laid on top. In terms of softness and hardness, pastel pencils lie somewhere in the middle. The colour ranges are similar to those of hard pastels.

OIL PASTELS

These can't be used in combination with ordinary pastels, as they are bound with oil rather than gum. They are, however, an excellent alternative to soft pastels and are capable of very exciting and painterly effects. What is particularly intriguing about them is that the colour can be "melted" with turpentine or white spirit, then spread across the paper with a brush. You can even dip a brush moistened with turpentine into the sticks of colour and apply it, just as you would put on paint. The colours are rather more restricted than those of soft pastels but, as the medium grows in popularity, manufacturers are beginning to respond to demand.

DIFFERENT SHADES

In oil, watercolour and acrylic painting, you can manage with very few basic colours because you can obtain so many more by means of mixing. Pastels, however, can't be premixed, so you will need many more sticks of pastel than you would tubes of paint. Choosing a range of colours which gives you sufficient scope for colour matching, without incurring vast expense, can be a problematical business. Some ranges contain literally hundreds of colours, so where do you start?

Fortunately many manufacturers help you here, producing "starter" sets tailored to particular subject areas. There are, for example, large and small boxed sets, with a range of suitable colours for either landscape or portrait work. One of these

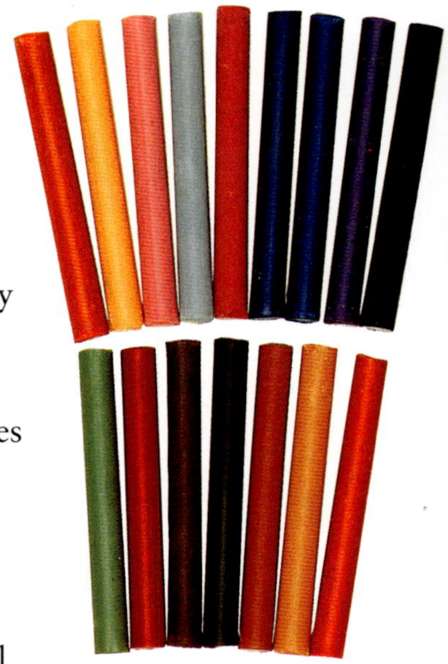

OIL PASTELS

PASTEL PENCILS

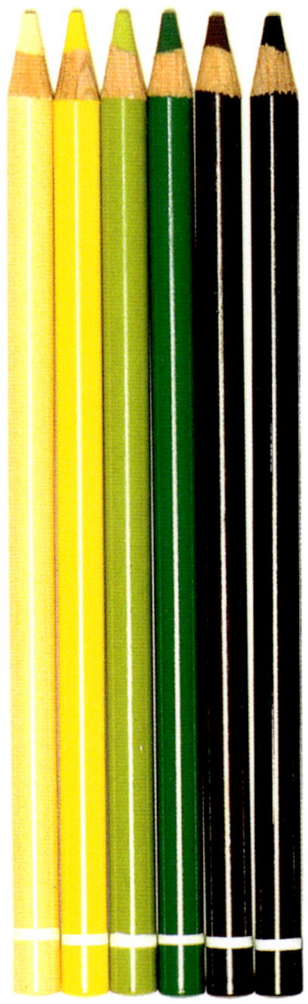

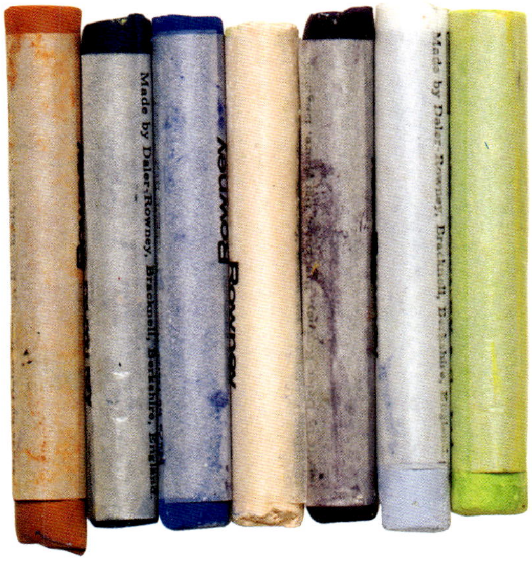

SOFT PASTELS

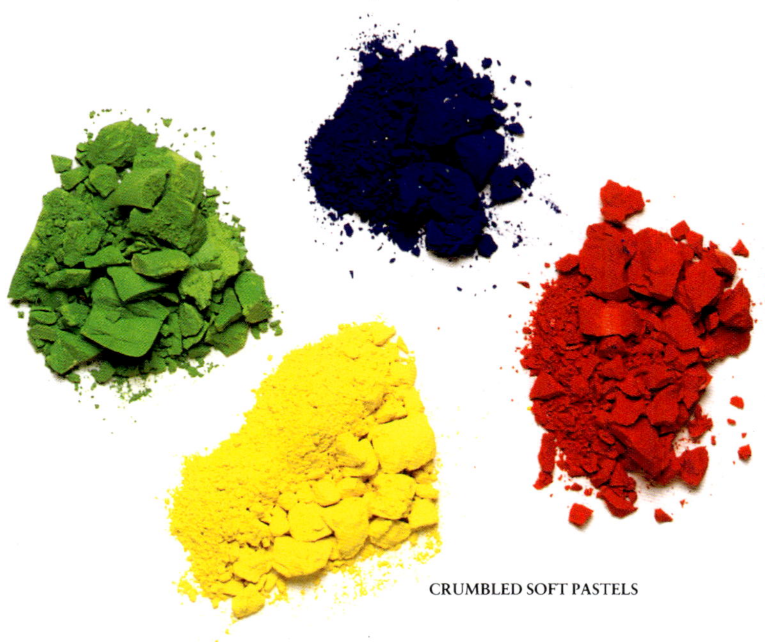

CRUMBLED SOFT PASTELS

could make a good starting point. You can add more colours when you know which ones you need – all pastels are sold singly as well as in boxes.

If you already know something about colour, you can simply rely on choosing by eye. As you look through drawers of pastels, you will notice that some of the colours bear a name and a number. The latter denotes the tone of the colour, whether it is a light or dark version of ultramarine, for example. All pastel colours are made in a pure hue plus light and dark versions, the former achieved by adding white and the latter by adding black. Unfortunately, there is no standard naming or numbering system among manufacturers but, as you become more experienced, you will be able to pick out the colours you want quite quickly.

Variations

There are considerable differences in colour from one range of pastels to another so, when you have reached the stage of adding colours, it's always worth trying out several different kinds. Experienced artists become familiar with the different ranges and often have one or two favourite colours made only by one particular manufacturer. They will thus have a selection of different makes in their "paintbox".

The textures vary too. Some "soft" pastels are relatively hard, while others are so crumbly that they break as soon as you pick them up and have to be spread with your fingers. You can find these things out only by experience, but it's all part of the learning process.

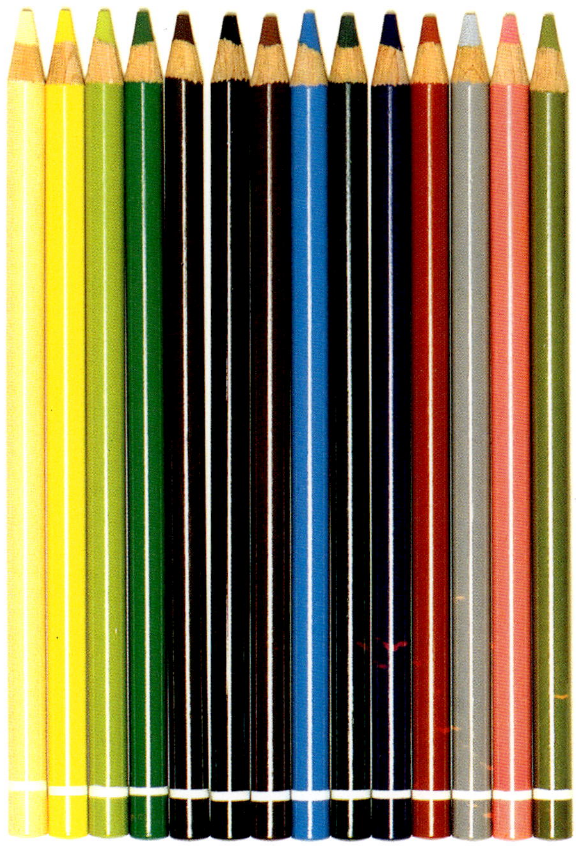

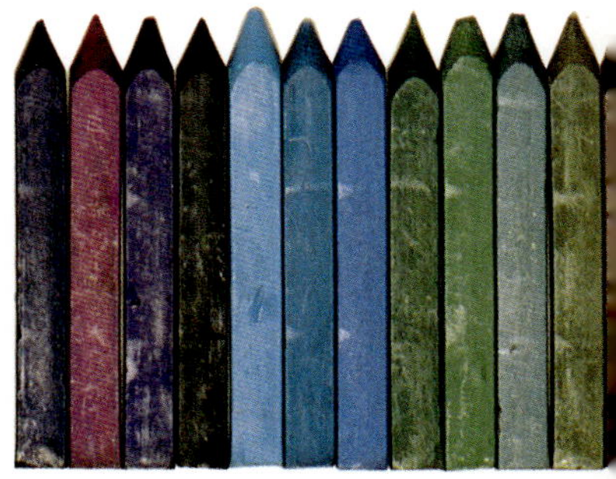

HARD PASTELS

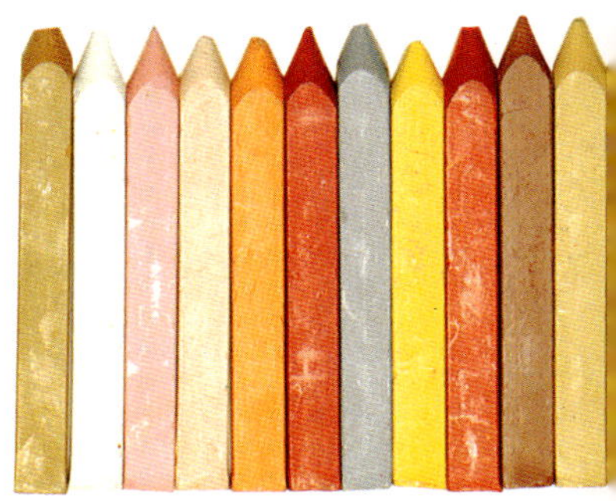

PASTEL PENCILS

PAPERS

The choice of paper is extremely important in pastel work because both the colour and the texture play an important part in the overall effect. Pastels are usually done on a coloured surface; the paper must also have some texture in order to hold the pigment (this is known as "tooth"). If you work on too smooth a surface, the pigment will tend to slip about and fall off, making it impossible to achieve any layering of colour in your picture.

PAPER AND TEXTURE SHADE

The reason for working on coloured paper is that it is very difficult, sometimes impossible, to cover the whole surface with pastel. Even if you use a pastel stick fairly heavily on its side, some of the paper will still show through. Small flecks of white paper appearing between pastel strokes create a jumpy effect, as well as devaluing the colours. Thus it is usual to work on a colour that either complements or tones in with the overall colour scheme of the picture. There are artists who like to work on white paper, but they are very much in the minority.

There are two standard papers made for pastel work: Ingres and Mi-Teintes (these are not manufacturers' names; they describe a type of paper). Both are made in a wide range of colours and both have a texture to hold the pigment in place. Ingres is a laid paper, with a pattern of fine, even lines, while Mi-Teintes has a pattern of dots slightly resembling fine chicken wire. It is worth trying both of these, as you will only discover which one you like best by hands-on experience. You can also use the "wrong" side of Mi-Teintes paper if you find the grain too obtrusive.

The choice of colour is more difficult, as it involves knowing what your picture will look like before you start. Some artists choose a paper which will be one of the key colours in the painting, and leave areas of it

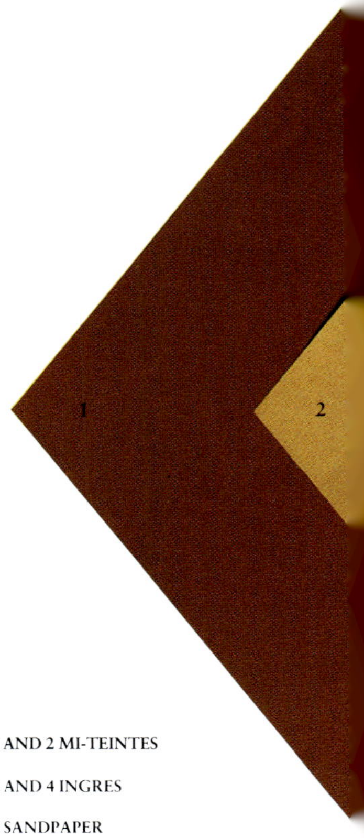

1 AND 2 MI-TEINTES
3 AND 4 INGRES
5 SANDPAPER
6 AND 7 SANSFIX PAPER
8 WATERCOLOUR PAPER

FIXATIVE

Although some artists dislike fixative and use it as little as possible or even not at all, you will certainly need it when you are starting out in pastel. Unless you can frame and glaze your pictures immediately, there is a serious risk of smudging them if you fail to spray them with fixative before putting them away. Even after fixing, you will still need a sheet of tissue paper on top of the picture to protect it.

The problem with fixative is that it does tend to darken the colours slightly; you may also lose something of the delicate, fragile texture of pastel pigment. However, for any painting built up thickly in layers, it is essential to spray at regular stages, in order to overwork with new colours without disturbing earlier ones. Keep the spray as light as you can – several sparing applications are better than one heavy one – and don't continue working until you are sure the fixative is completely dry.

You can either use a bottle of fixative with a mouth diffuser or an aerosol can; the latter are all now "ozone friendly" and produce a suitably fine spray. They are quite expensive, however, so you might like to consider using odourless hairspray as an alternative – the ingredients are much the same.

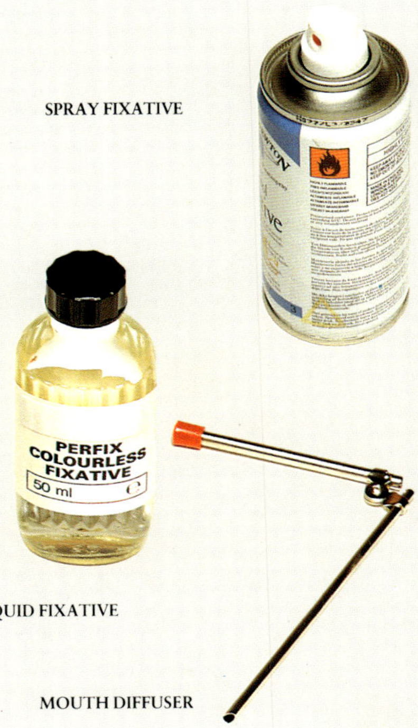

SPRAY FIXATIVE

LIQUID FIXATIVE

MOUTH DIFFUSER

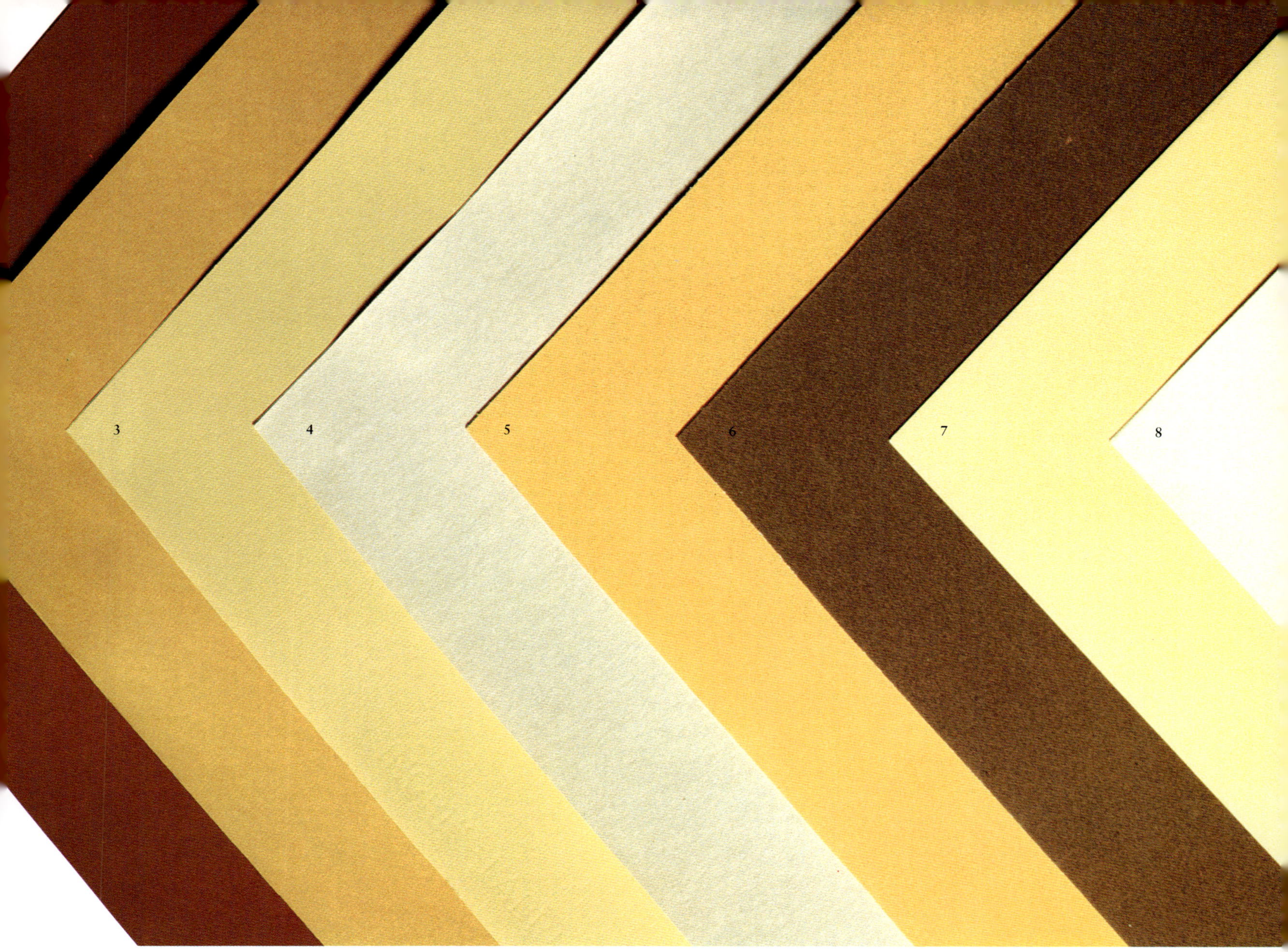

uncovered. For example, a blue-grey might be chosen for a landscape or seascape seen under a cloudy sky, with parts of the paper left for areas of sky and water. Other artists like to work on a contrasting colour, choosing, for example, yellow for a snow scene consisting mainly of blues and blue-greys. To start with, it is probably best to choose a neutral mid-toned colour such as light grey or beige; very bright or very dark colours are hard to manage until you know what you are doing.

Other papers

You can also work on a variety of papers not actually designed for pastel work, such as medium (Not surface) watercolour paper (CP paper). This has a very pronounced texture, which breaks up the pastel strokes, while also allowing for heavy build-ups of colour. If you use watercolour paper, you can tint it in advance by laying a watercolour wash. There are also three special papers produced for pastels, used by artists who like to build up colours very thickly: sandpaper, velour paper and Sansfix paper.

Sandpaper is the same as the fine sandpaper sold for carpentry and other work around the home, but the artist's version comes in much larger sheets. Velour paper, as its name implies, has a velvety texture and gives an attractive soft line. The third alternative, Sansfix (also called Rembrandt paper depending on who makes it), is similar to sandpaper but slightly less abrasive. There is no need for fixative when using any of these papers.

Line Strokes

Pastel is a drawing medium as well as a painting one, in as much as the pastel stick, like a pencil, is the direct intermediary between your hand and the paper. Although it is possible to produce a pastel painting in which all the colours are smoothly blended and there are no visible lines or marks, this is something of a lost opportunity, as the way in which pastel bridges the gap between drawing and painting is one of its major attractions. In the 18th century, when pastel painting became very popular, artists such as Jean-Etienne Liotard and Maurice Quentin de La Tour produced works whose smooth finishes emulated contemporary oil paintings. However, nowadays most artists prefer to exploit the mark-making aspect of pastel, to give free rein to its energetic, linear quality.

In order to do this successfully, you will need to develop your own "handwriting" in pastel. The tip of a pastel stick can produce a wide variety of different marks, depending on the pressure you apply, the sharpness or bluntness of the point and how you hold the stick. To practise mark-making, don't try to draw actual objects, but just doodle or scribble as the mood takes you. Try applying heavy pressure at the start of a line and then tapering off towards the end, or twisting the stick in mid-stroke so that it trails off in a narrow tail.

Although pastel is soft and crumbly, you will find that you can make surprisingly fine lines if you break a stick in half and use the edge of the broken end. However, hard pastels are the ones for really crisp details, so if you have these in addition to soft pastels, experiment with them too.

Side strokes

The way to cover large areas of the paper in pastel painting is to sweep the side of the stick across the paper, thus depositing a

(Below) *These swatches show the variety of marks that you can make with the tip and side of a pastel stick.*

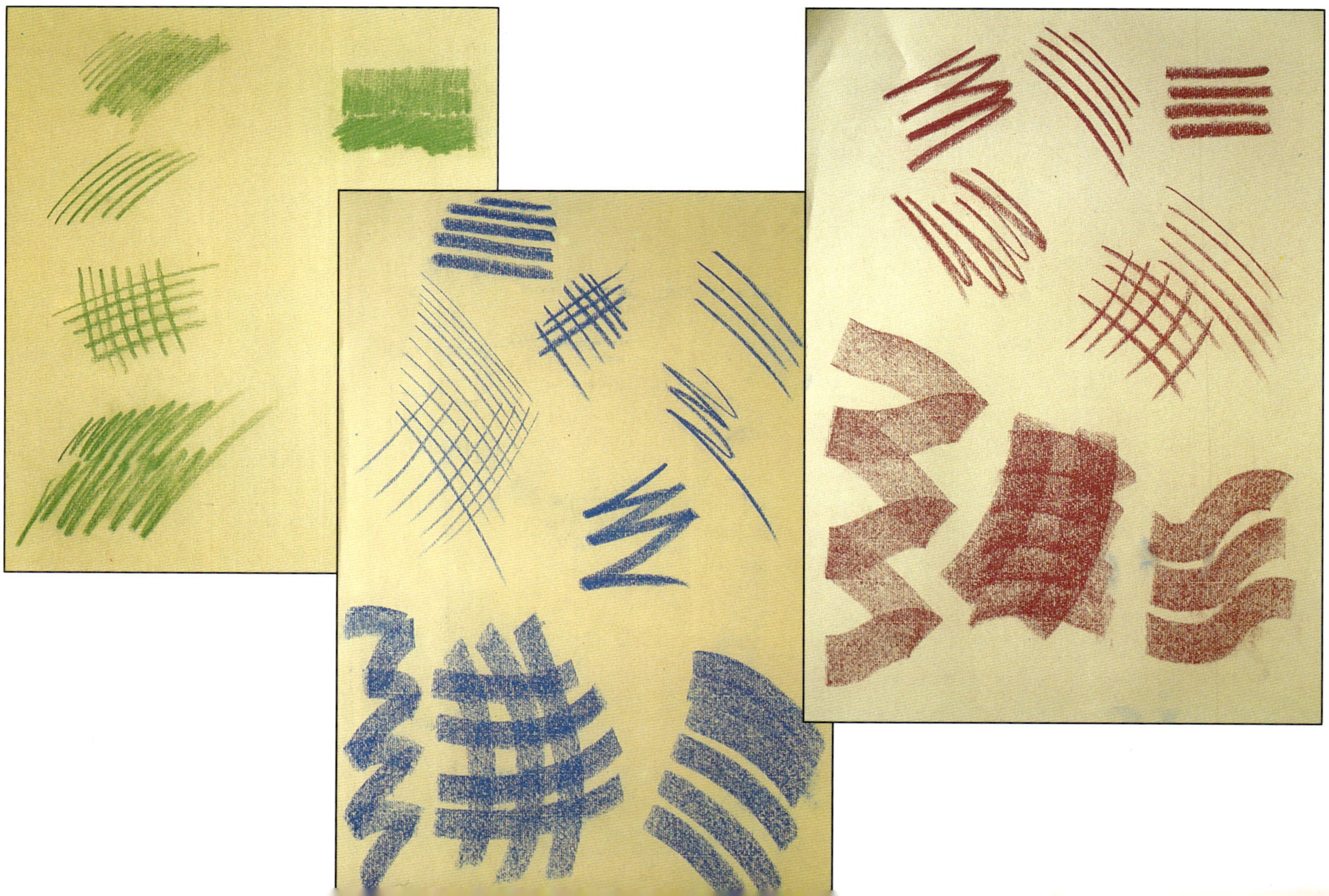

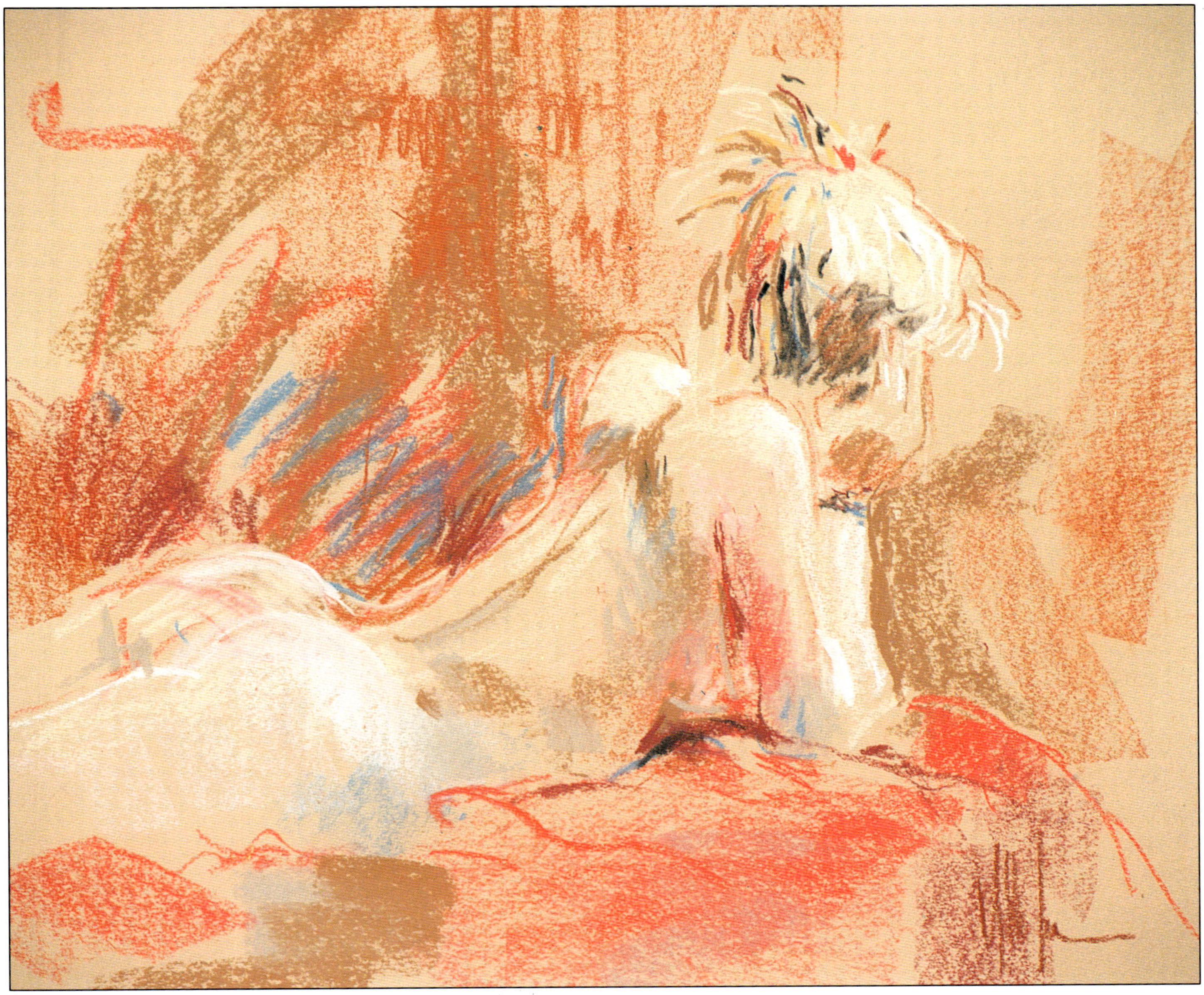

MAUREEN JORDAN
NUDE AGAINST PINK
A classic combination of line and side strokes can be seen in this lively figure study. Notice how the artist has used the pastel sticks in a descriptive way, following the directions of the shapes and forms.

broad band of colour. Side strokes can, however, be much more than just a means of "blocking in" – they can be as varied, beautiful and expressive as line strokes. Many different effects can be created by varying the pressure and direction of the stroke, by laying one stroke over another, by blending in some areas and by laying one colour over another.

The length of the pastel stick also affects the kind of stroke you make. Unless you are using hard pastels, which are relatively tough, you will nearly always have to break the stick. If you try to make side strokes with the whole length of the stick, it will probably break under pressure anyway, added to which a short length is more controllable. Usually the length should not be more than 5 cm (2 in), but you can use much smaller pieces of pastel than these to make short, jabbing strokes, similar to linear marks.

The other factor which affects side strokes, even more than linear ones, is the texture of the paper. A heavy texture such as watercolour paper will break up the stroke, producing a grainy effect, with the colour deposited only on the top of the weave. On smoother paper, the colour will be denser and, if you apply the pastel heavily, it will cover the paper thoroughly. Be warned that, if you intend to use side strokes as a means of colour mixing, with one colour laid over another, the pressure should be kept light initially, or the paper will quickly become clogged.

MIXING PASTELS

However many pastels you have – and professional pastel painters may have hundreds – you will nearly always have to mix them to reproduce the colours you see. Nature provides far more subtle and varied nuances of colour than could be matched by any manufacturer of artist's pigments.

LIGHTENING AND DARKENING COLOURS

As mentioned earlier, all pastel colours are made in light and dark versions. Further variations of tone (the lightness and darkness of colours) are produced by controlling the amount of pressure you apply to the pastel stick – the heavier the pressure, the more solid the colour will be. However, you will frequently have to lighten or darken colours by mixing. A pale blue sky, for example, may call for a combination of blue and white, or blue and pale grey; dark areas of foliage or heavy shadows may need a mixture of dark blue or black with green and other colours. Black is particularly useful in pastel work as the colours are brilliant and generally not very dark, so it is hard to achieve any depth of colour without using black.

METHODS OF MIXING

One of the best-known techniques for colour mixing is blending. Two or more colours are applied to the working surface and rubbed together with your fingers, a rag, a piece of cotton wool or an implement called a torchon (a rolled paper stump made specially for the purpose). If you choose your pastel sticks carefully, you can achieve almost any colour and tone in this way. However, although blending is ideal for areas of a picture where you want a soft effect, you should not rely on it too much, as over-blending gives a bland impression.

Lightening

1 When very pale pastel colours are required, it is sometimes necessary to mix on the paper surface by adding white. Here white is laid over a mid-blue.

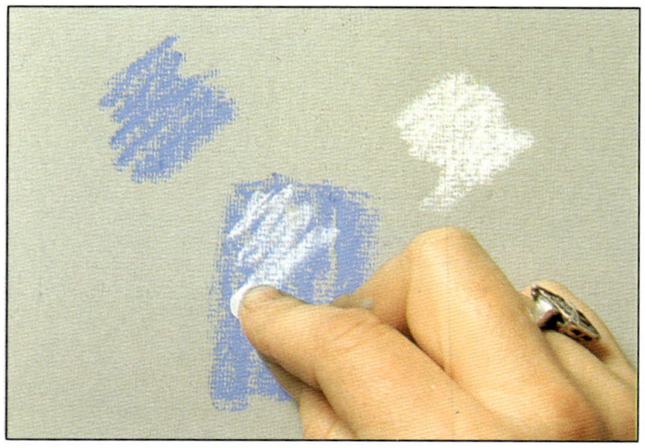

2 The pastel pigments are gently blended together with a finger-tip. Be prepared to use your fingers a good deal in pastel work; they are the best "implements" for blending in relatively small areas.

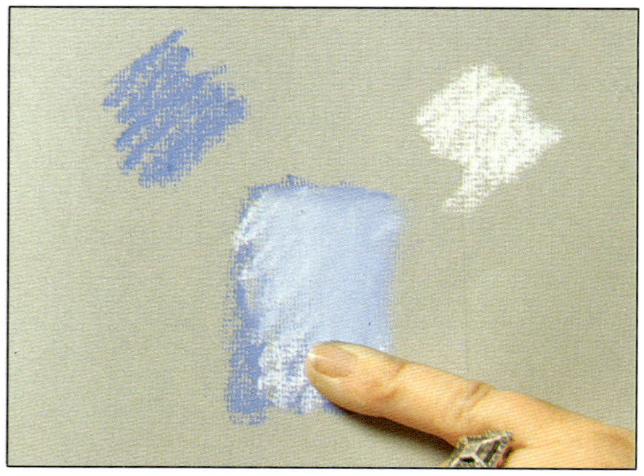

Darkening

1 Black is a useful colour in pastel work, as it can be difficult to achieve really dark colours without it. Here the black is laid down first, with the green on top.

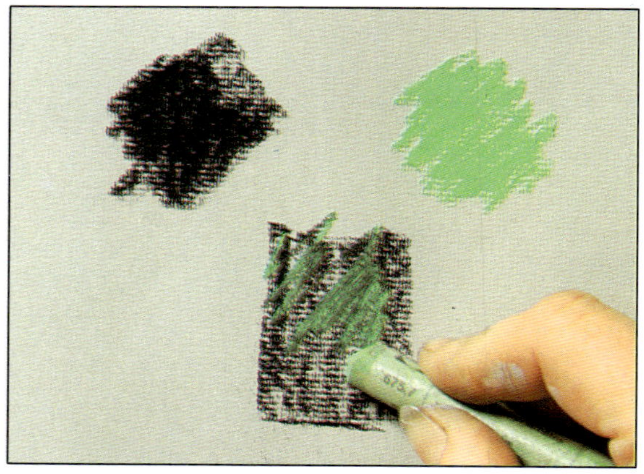

2 With experience you will discover which colours can be successfully darkened with black. In this case, the mixture is rather muddy and the light green has lost much of its character.

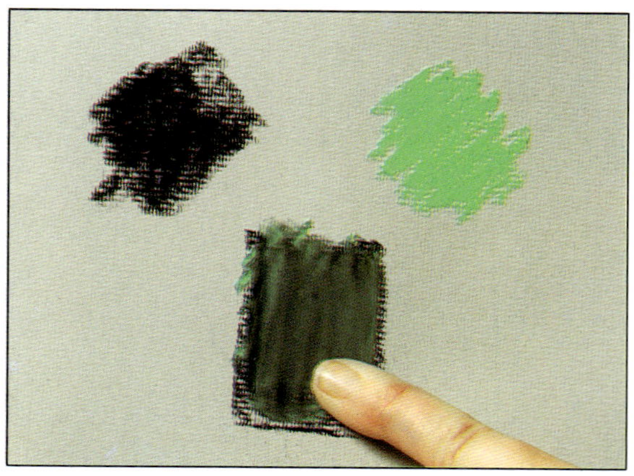

Mixing greens

To reproduce the wide range of greens in nature, you generally need to mix colours to some extent. Here, ultramarine is laid over a lemony yellow. The two colours are blended lightly to produce a strong green. Yellows and blues can also be added to ready-made greens to modify them.

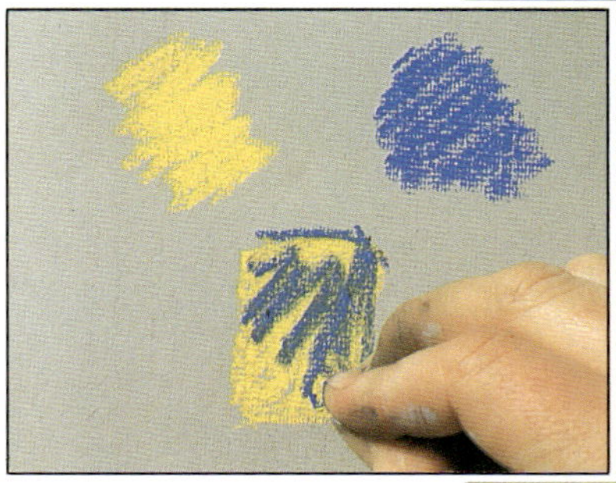

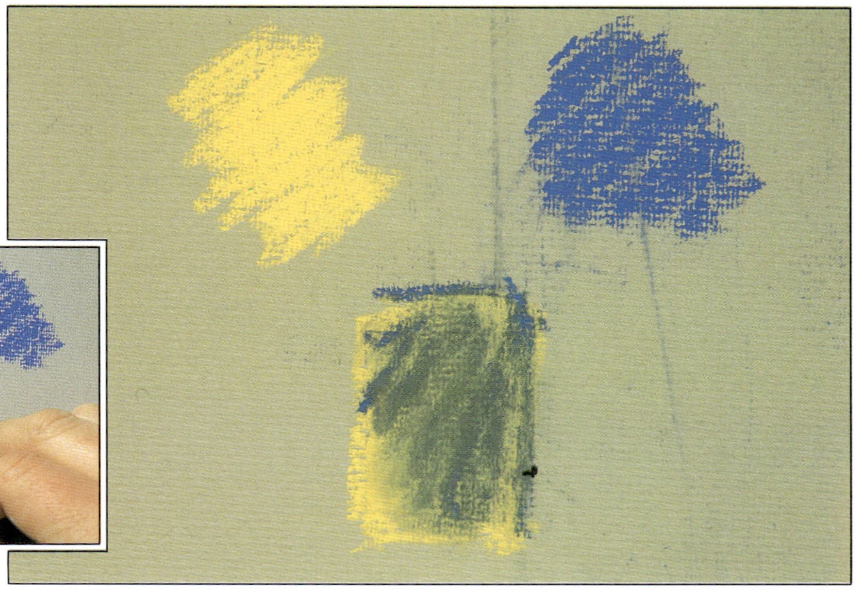

Mixing oranges

To mix a pure orange, choose the strongest red and yellow in your pastel set, and lay the yellow over the red. Even when the two colours are blended, the darker colour will dominate if it is laid over the lighter one. Experiment to discover the effect of light-over-dark and dark-over-light mixtures.

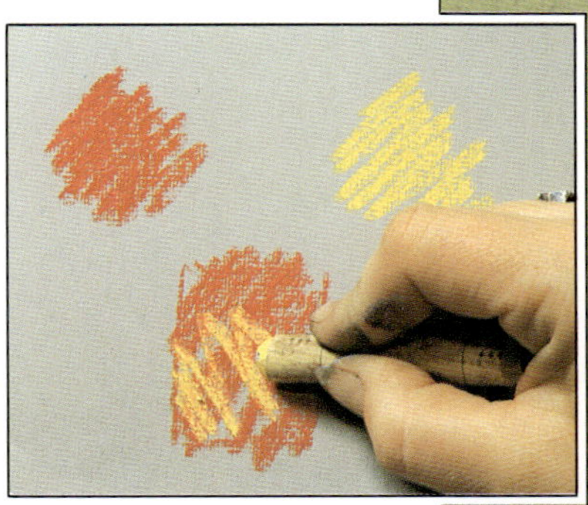

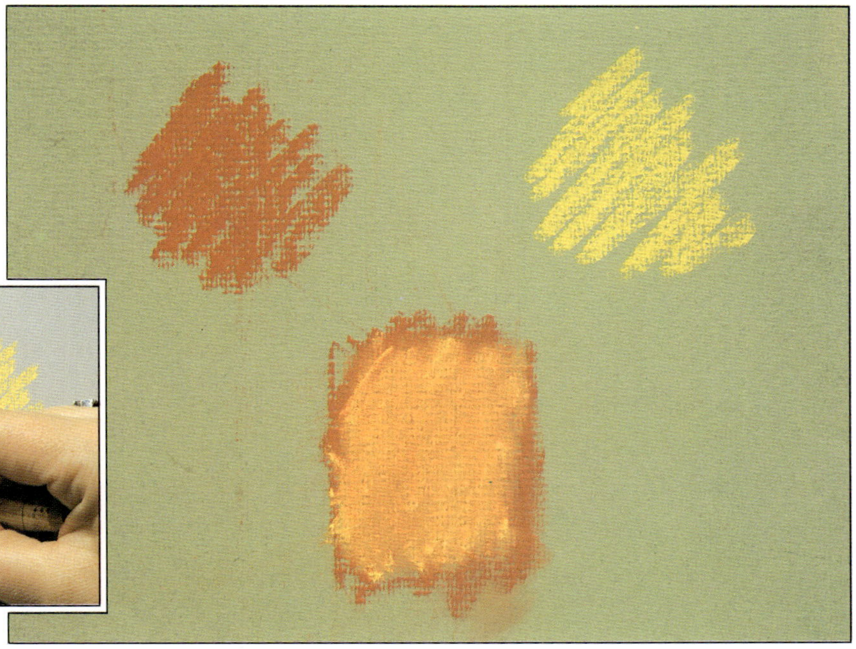

Mixing greys

Most pastel ranges include a good selection of greys, but they can easily be mixed from black and white. Other colours, such as blues and greens, can be added for interest. The result will be affected by the order in which the colours are laid: white over black will produce a lighter mixture, particularly if the colours are only blended gently.

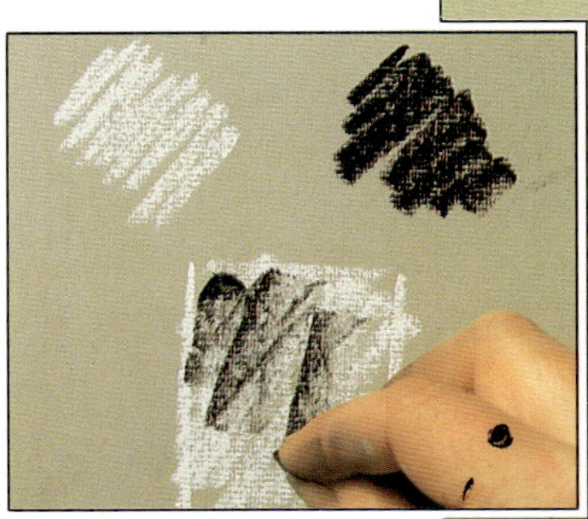

Blending large areas

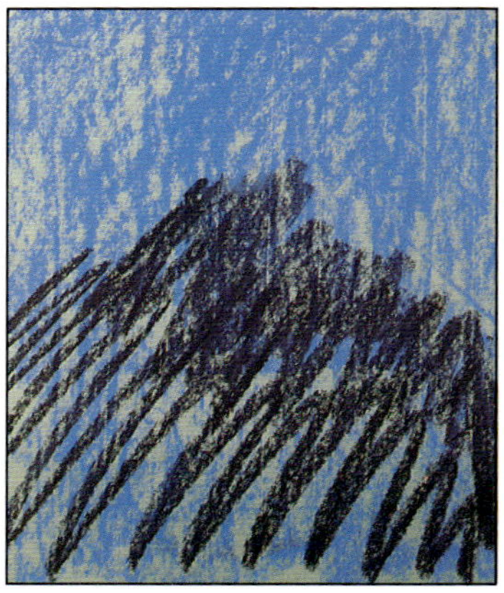

1 *For a subtle blend which would be suitable for a large area of sky, blue and black are first lightly scribbled together.*

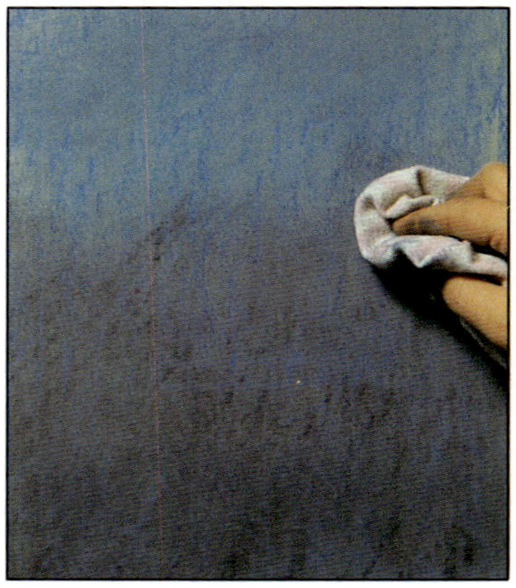

2 *The rag used to blend the colours knocks some of the particles of pastel off the paper, producing a lighter mixture than finger blending, which pushes the pigment into the paper.*

Feathering

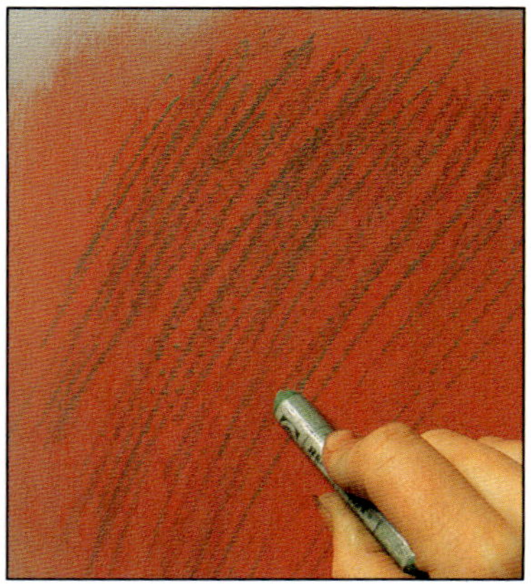

This is a useful method for rejuvenating an area of colour which has become flat and dull, or for toning down an over-bright colour. Here light feathering strokes are made in green over an area of red.

A light, unblended application of one colour over another makes a more vibrant and exciting alternative because the first colour shows through the second, producing an attractive sparkle. Pastels are opaque, and so light colours can be laid over dark ones as well as the other way round, to modify the tone of colours.

For many artists, one of the main attractions of pastel is its vigorous linear quality, with the marks of the pastel stick forming an integral part of the image (like brushwork in painting). For this reason, colours are sometimes mixed by building up a network of linear strokes which merge when seen from a distance. A related method is feathering, which is often used to revive an area of colour which has become flat and dull through over-zealous blending. It involves dragging light strokes of colour over the offending area with the tip of the pastel stick and provides a useful means of modifying colours which do not look quite right. For example, a solid area of red which seems too bright in the overall context of your painting can be feathered over lightly with strokes of green, or a too-blue sky can be transformed with greys or pale mauves.

CHOOSING PAPER

When one colour is laid over another it produces a third colour – yellow over blue makes green; red over yellow makes orange and so on. Thus it follows that the colour of the paper will influence the applied colour. If you choose a neutral mid-toned paper the effect will not be dramatic, but a light application of yellow on a rich blue paper has a similar effect to laying yellow over blue pastel. It is important to remember this, as the paper always acts as a third colour in any two-colour mixture, unless the pastel is applied heavily. On the following pages you can see some of the effects of the paper colour on mixtures.

GEOFF MARSTERS
FEN LIGHT
(Above) *Rich painterly effects have been achieved by laying one colour over another, with the work fixed between stages. For the bright patches of highlight in the fields, the artist has used the tips of the pastel sticks, applying thick colour over softer blends.*

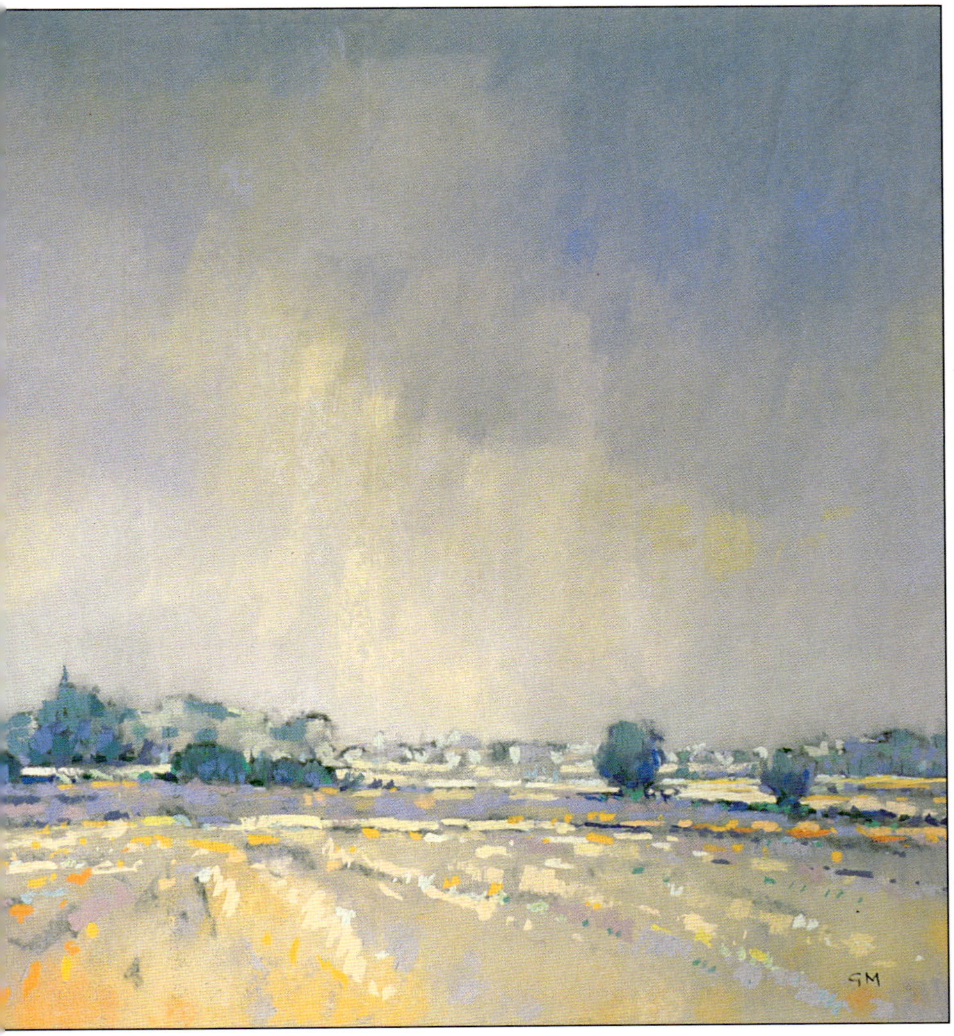

Using the paper colour

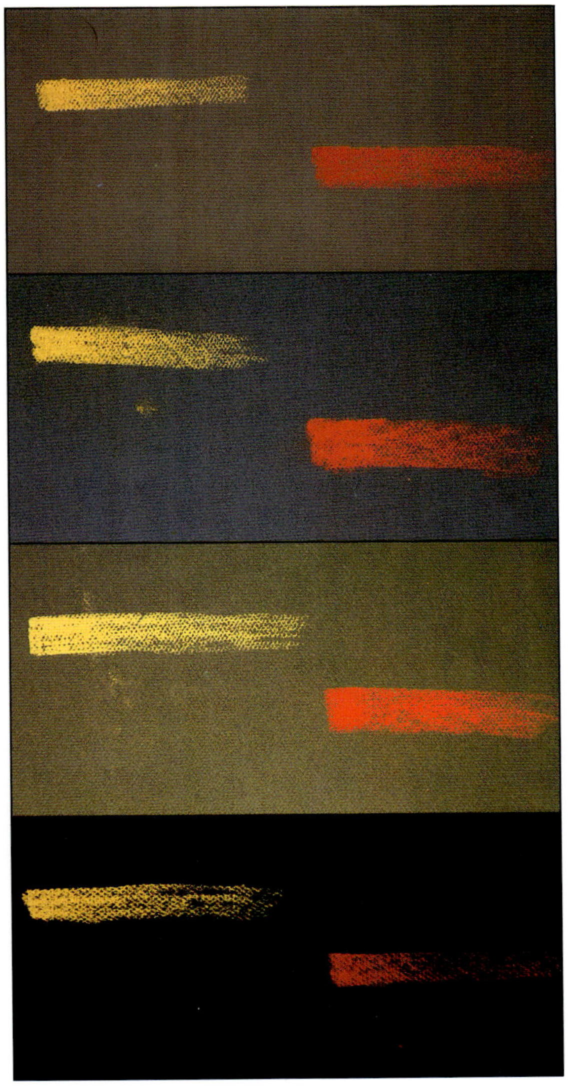

(Above) *As you can see in these examples, even when pastel is applied thickly, small specks of the paper will show through, affecting the appearance of the applied colour. The colour of the paper also influences the way you work, acting as the "key" against which you must judge the first colours you put on. Working on black or very dark blue paper makes it difficult to assess the lighter colours, because even a brilliant green or red will look pale in comparison. Until you have gained some experience, it is wise to choose a mid-toned neutral colour, thus avoiding the possibility of the base colour working against you.*

Overlays

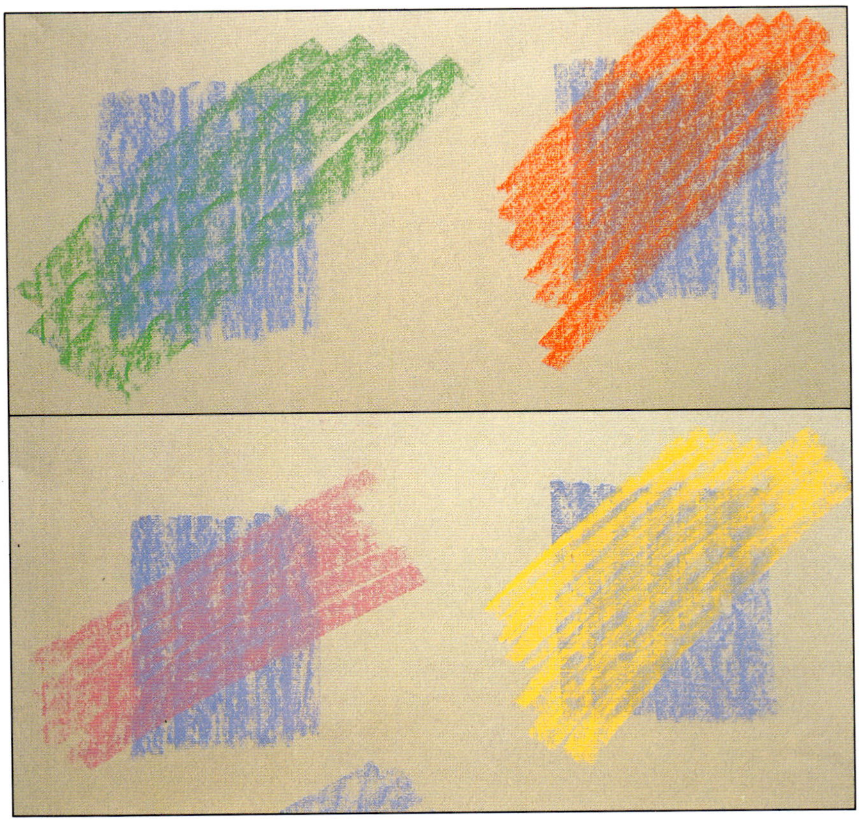

(Left) *Thoroughly blended colour mixtures may be necessary in certain areas of a painting, but the effects of unblended colours are often more exciting. In these examples you can see how one colour shows through another to produce a lively, sparkling effect.*

Exercise: Experimenting with Different Papers

It requires a good deal of experience to know which colour of paper to choose, so it is not a bad idea to start by painting the same subject on two different colours. Set up a simple still-life group, making sure that whatever objects you choose have a predominant colour theme. You might decide on blue, in which case you could paint a bunch of blue flowers, perhaps with one or two yellow ones for contrast. Or you might set up a still life consisting of green bottles, again with one other colour for contrast – perhaps an orange or apple.

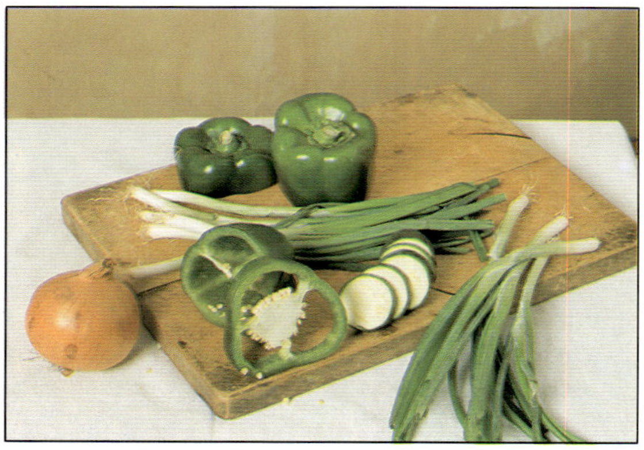

Paint the still life first on a colour which is the opposite of the main colour in the group. This is orange-yellow if you have chosen blue as the predominant colour, and red or red-brown if you have decided on green. These opposite colours are called complementaries; there are three pairs of them: red and green, blue and orange, and yellow and violet. For your second painting, choose a paper which represents one of the colours in the subject. For the blue flower group you could use a dark or mid-toned blue, or a blue-grey. You should find that you don't have to cover the entire paper with pastel colour.

Some artists always use a complementary coloured paper, while others prefer one which tones with the key subject colour.

Painting on toning paper

1 Working on dark green paper, chosen in order to represent the dominant greens of the still life, the artist begins with the opposite colour, making a light drawing in red-brown pastel.

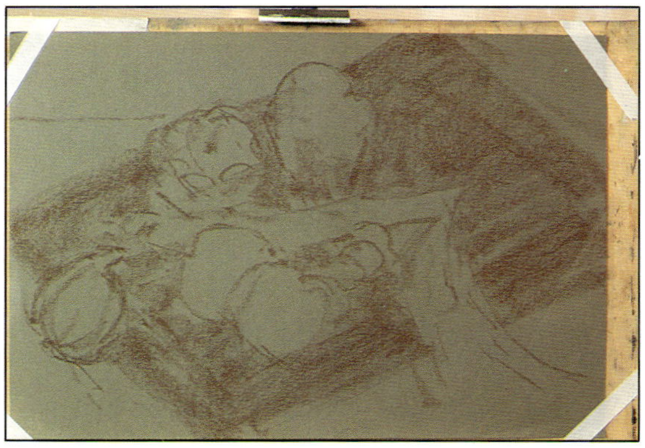

2 Initially, she concentrates on covering the green paper in the non-green areas, establishing the contrasting warm browns and blue-whites. Notice that she does not attempt to cover the paper entirely; the paper colour still shows through.

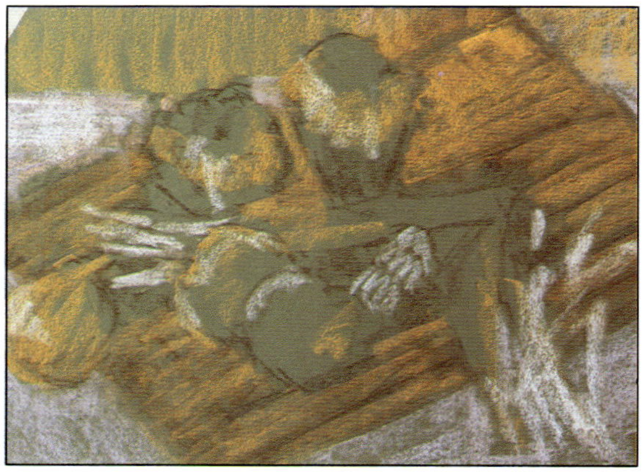

Painting on contrasting paper

1 In this case the paper picks up the yellow-brown of the board, but is in opposition to the greens of the vegetables.

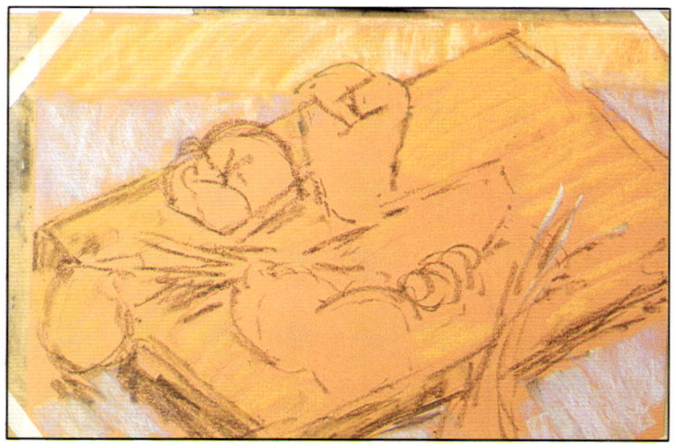

2 To counteract the colour of the paper, the artist has to use a different selection of greens and yellows from those she chose for the first painting. Here the colour scheme is warmer and the greens are also less dominant.

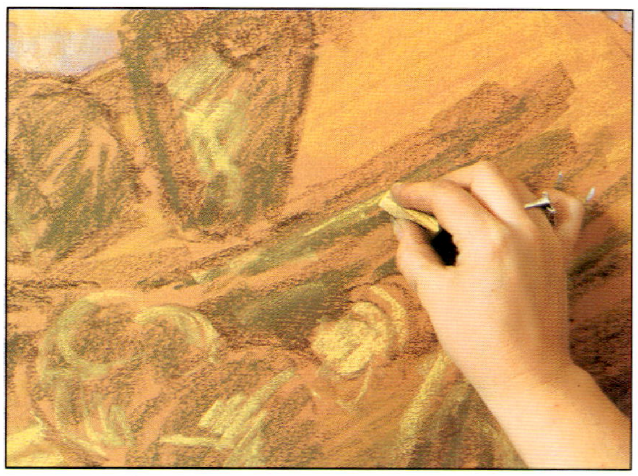

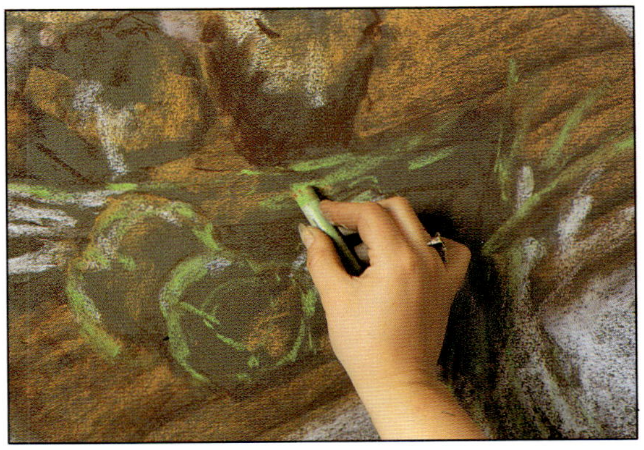

3 *Leaving the paper colour to stand for the mid-tones of the vegetables, she now builds up both the dark shadows (the pepper in the background) and the brighter green highlights. Touches of the warm browns and yellows used for the chopping board have also been introduced into the vegetables, so that the green-brown theme runs through the picture.*

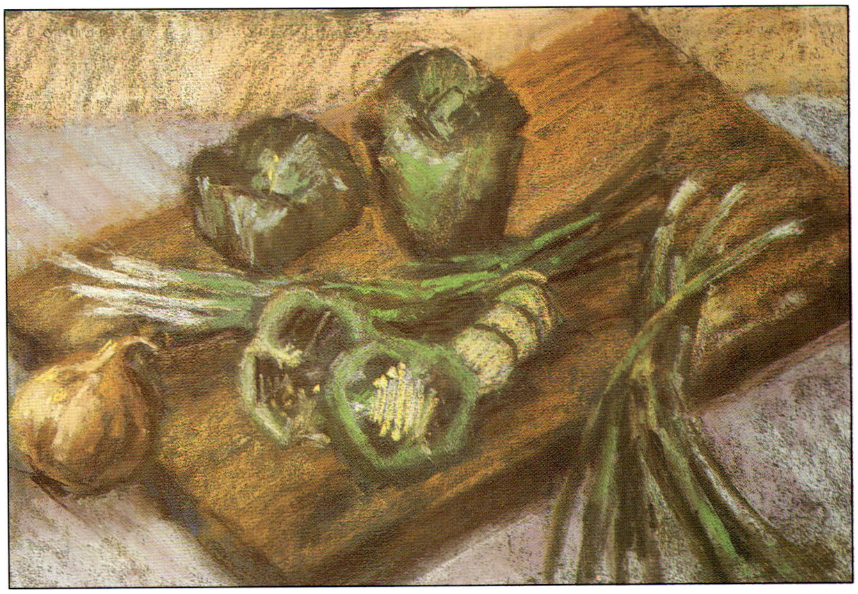

4 *The finished picture shows the importance of the role played by the colour of the paper. Large areas have been left uncovered on the vegetables; elsewhere in the painting, streaks and flecks of the green base colour show through the light pastel strokes. Repeating colours from one part of a picture in another area makes a series of visual links, creating an overall unity in the composition.*

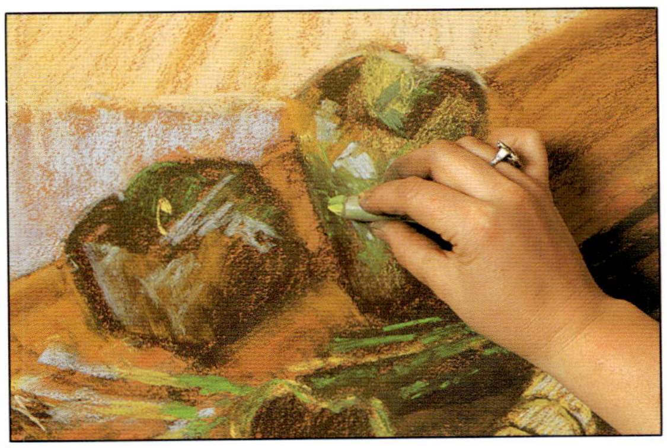

3 *In the first painting, the greens of the vegetables were applied quite lightly because the paper did not need to be covered completely. Here, however, the greens have to be built up heavily to prevent too much of the paper from showing through.*

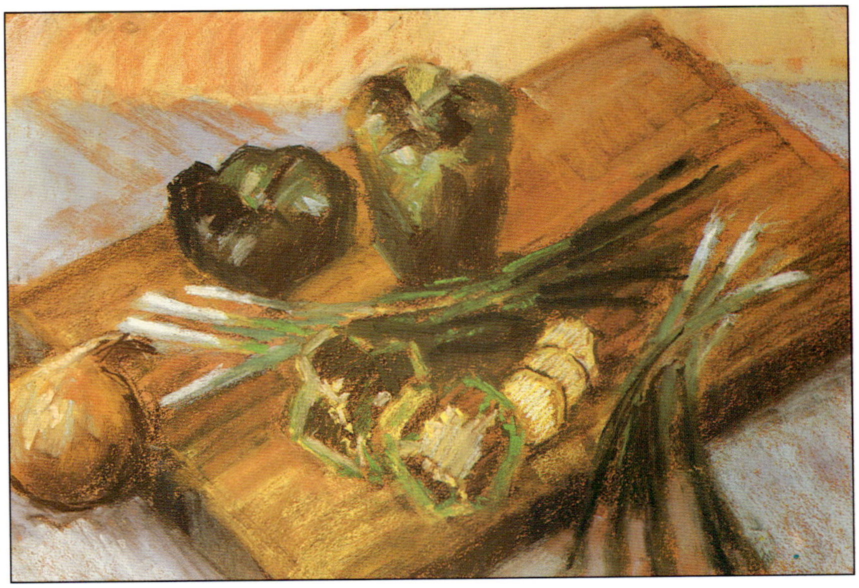

4 *There are a number of differences between this and the first painting. The dominant colour here is orange-brown rather than green, with the paper colour showing through most clearly on the board and in the background. The method of working has also been affected by the need to build up the greens heavily; the vegetables look darker and more solid, forming a stronger contrast with the wooden board. Both paintings are on the "wrong" – smoother – side of Mi-Teintes paper, chosen in preference to the more obtrusive texture of the "right" side.*

TINTING YOUR PAPER

The two standard pastel papers, Ingres and Mi-Teintes, are produced in a vast range of colours. However, some artists, particularly those who like to build up their colours thickly, prefer to work on watercolour paper, which has a distinctive texture, and which they generally tint in advance with their chosen colour.

LAYING A TINTED GROUND

There are two ways of doing this. One is by laying a wash, either of watercolour or thinned acrylic paint, which is quick and easy. However, if you work exclusively in pastel you won't have these paints to hand, in which case you can prepare the paper with what is called a dry wash of pastel. To do this you first reduce a pastel stick to dust by holding it over a bowl or plate and scraping the long edge with a sharp knife. When you have sufficient colour, simply dip a piece of cotton wool (a cotton ball) or a rag into it and spread it over the paper surface, using an even pressure.

If you want an all-over colour, spread the pastel dust evenly across the paper. This method also allows you to introduce tonal variations by applying the colour more thickly in some areas than others. You can also use more than one colour, perhaps using a blue dry wash for a sky in a landscape and a brown or yellow ochre one for the ground. Indeed, dry washing need not be restricted to colouring the ground or sky, it is also a useful method for creating hazy effects of soft colour. If you intend to work over the wash, however, spray it with fixative first. The advantage of the watercolour or acrylic method is that you need not do this.

Laying a dry wash

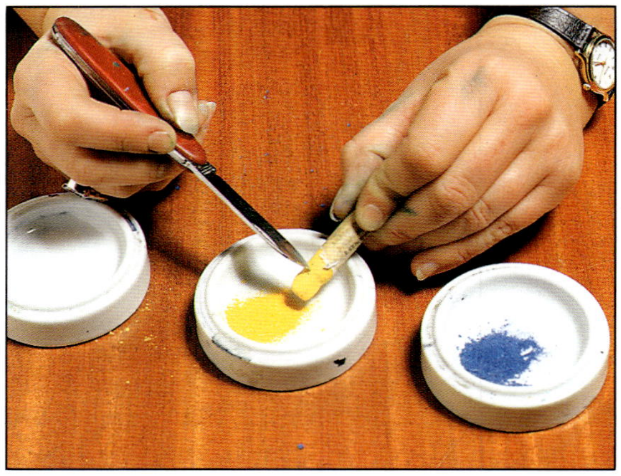

1 A knife is used to scrape the side of the pastel stick, producing a fine dust. The method may seem wasteful, but in fact you don't need a great deal of colour.

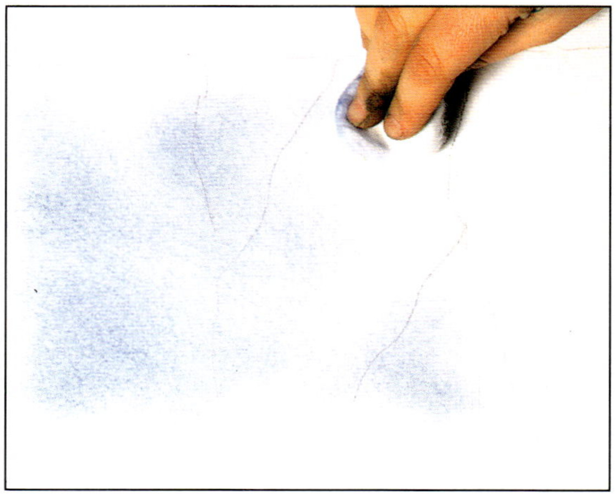

2 This dry wash is for a landscape, using two colours: blue for the sky and yellow for the land. The blue powder is applied lightly on watercolour paper with a piece of cotton wool (a cotton ball).

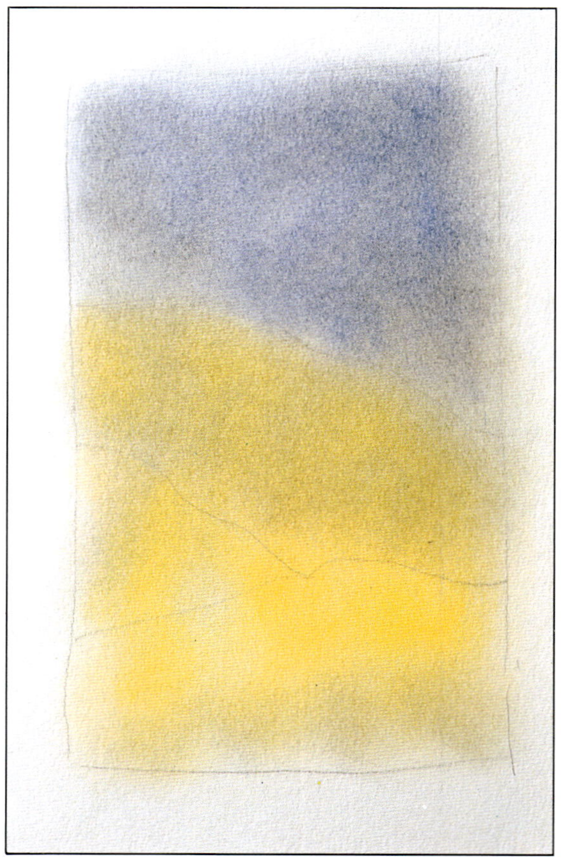

3 Some of the blue has been taken into the land area, and the yellow applied on top, so that the two colours overlap to produce a yellow-green mixture. Before starting the painting proper, the dry wash should be sprayed with fixative.

Wet brushing with a bristle brush

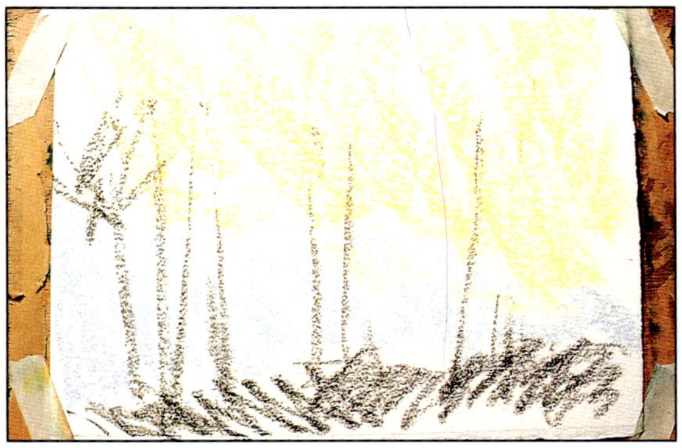

1 *Working on watercolour paper, the artist began by sketching out the composition. Having blocked in the large areas with side strokes, she then used a pastel tip to sketch in the shapes of the trees.*

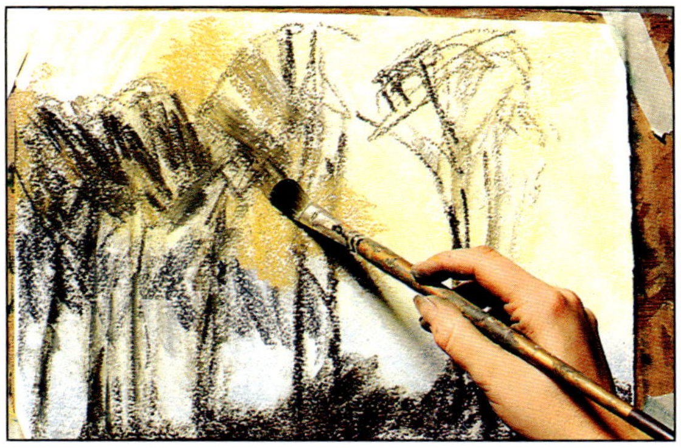

2 *A bristle brush dipped in water is used to spread the colour. This type of brush, being harder than a watercolour brush, creates a more thorough spread of colour, dislodging more particles.*

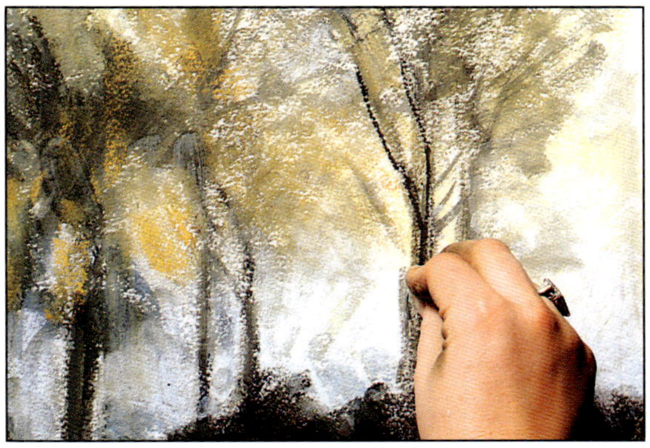

3 *She proceeds to draw over the wet-brushed areas with the tip of the pastel stick to add touches of crisp definition to the tree trunks and branches. In places, she has also drawn on still-damp paper to create softer lines and strokes.*

Wet brushing with a soft brush

Clean water taken over pastel marks with a soft brush releases some of the colour to form a watercolour effect, leaving the marks of the pastel stick intact. Watercolour paper rather than pastel paper should be used for this method, as the latter may buckle.

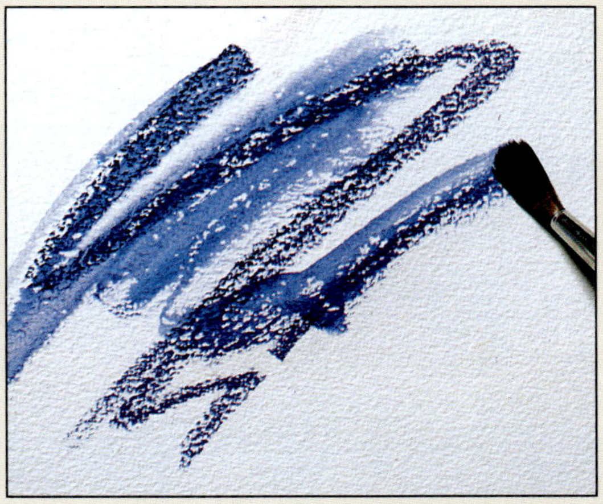

WET BRUSHING

If you go over soft pastel marks with a brush dipped in clean water, it releases some of the colour while leaving the pastel strokes clearly visible. You can use this technique only on watercolour paper, as the standard pastel papers are quite thin and would buckle under the water. If you like to work on watercolour paper, however, wet brushing forms a useful alternative to tinting the paper in advance. It allows you to cover the surface quickly with colour, obliterating the distracting white specks you see between strokes on white paper.

Wet brushing over side strokes produces a granular wash, which is ideal for suggesting the texture of objects such as rocks, cliffs or the barks of trees in a landscape. Over linear strokes, the effect is somewhat similar to that of line and wash in watercolour, with the wash a paler version of the original line. Wet brushing is often used to "pull together" lines and marks made with soft pastel or pastel pencil; it can also create light and shade effects to suggest form.

The idea of wetting pastel colour is not new. Edgar Degas, who took to pastel painting when his eyesight began to fail, was one of the greatest technical innovators in the medium. He would make a paste of his pastels, sometimes steaming his board or spraying warm water over the colours and then working into them with stiff brushes, before overlaying further linear marks.

UNDERPAINTING

The practice of working over an underpainting, usually done in either watercolour or acrylic, is rapidly gaining acceptance in pastel-painting circles. It stems from the same idea as colouring the paper in advance, but goes several steps further. By making a full-scale underpainting, you can introduce as many colours as you like before laying on any pastel, and so relate the colours to the shapes in your picture. Alternatively you can make a monochrome underpainting to establish the drawing and main tonal structure of the painting, perhaps choosing a colour which contrasts with the overall colour key of the subject.

The advantage of a multi-coloured underpainting is that you can carry out at least some of the colour mixing at the painting stage. This helps to avert one of the potential dangers of pastel painting: over-mixing and clogging the surface of the paper. You can also work on smoother paper than usual; as you will not be laying so many layers of pastel colour, there will be less risk of the pastel pigment slipping off the surface. As a general rule pastel paper should be textured, but it can be exciting to work on a smoother surface, such as Hot-pressed watercolour paper. This does not break up the pastel strokes as much as the medium-surface (Not, or CP) paper normally used for watercolour work, thus allowing you to lay thick, solid areas of smooth colour.

Pastel over paint

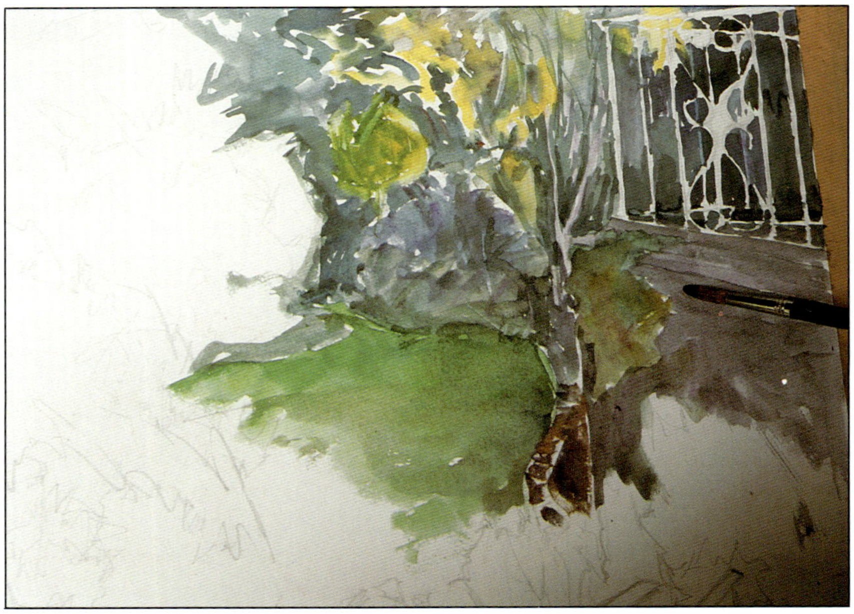

1 *Working on medium-surface watercolour paper, the artist begins with watercolour. He allows the brushmarks to show in order to complement the pastel strokes.*

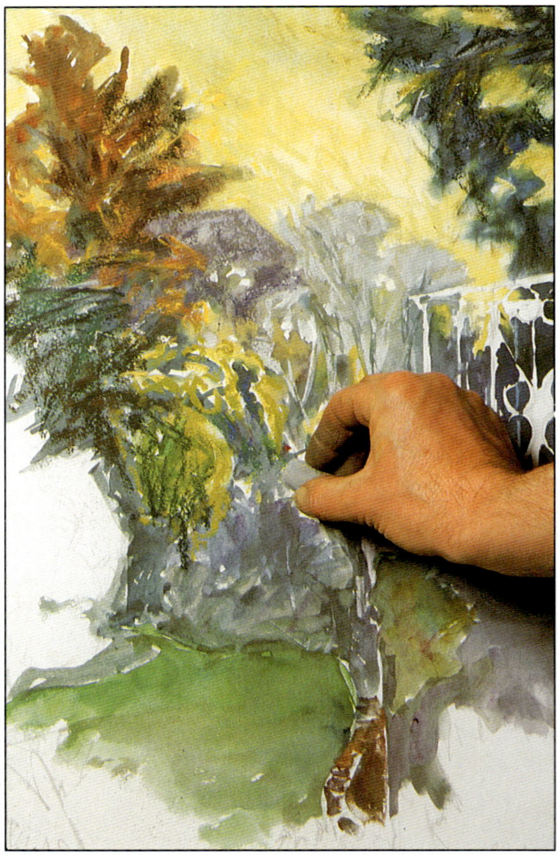

2 *Light pastel marks now overlay the paint in the foliage and sky areas, and pale grey is used to draw into the darker blue-greys.*

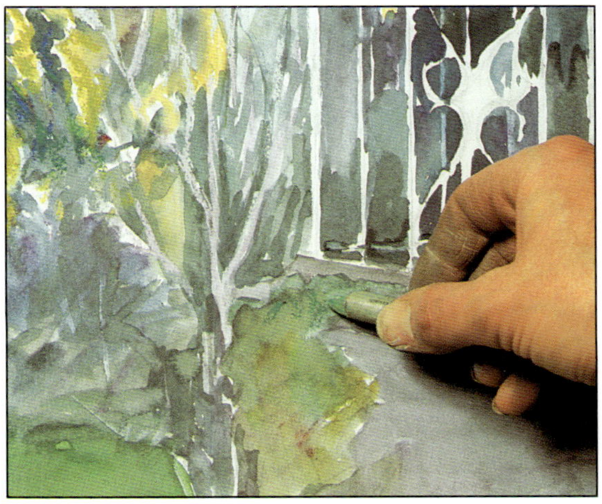

3 *As he wishes to achieve a blend of the two media, the pastel colours chosen are close to those of the watercolour beneath. There is no attempt to cover the first colours completely.*

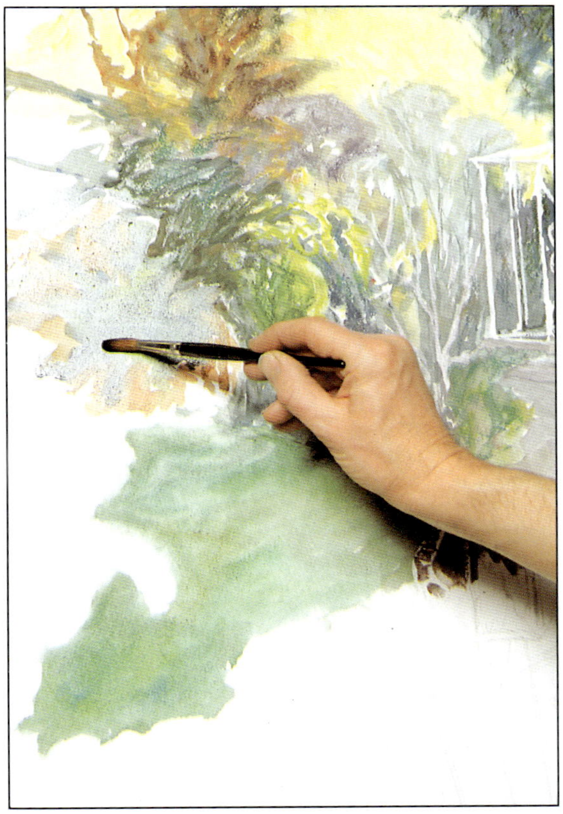

4 *The artist works from the centre of the picture outwards, and now lays down more watercolour, again using brushstrokes which suggest the movement of the foliage.*

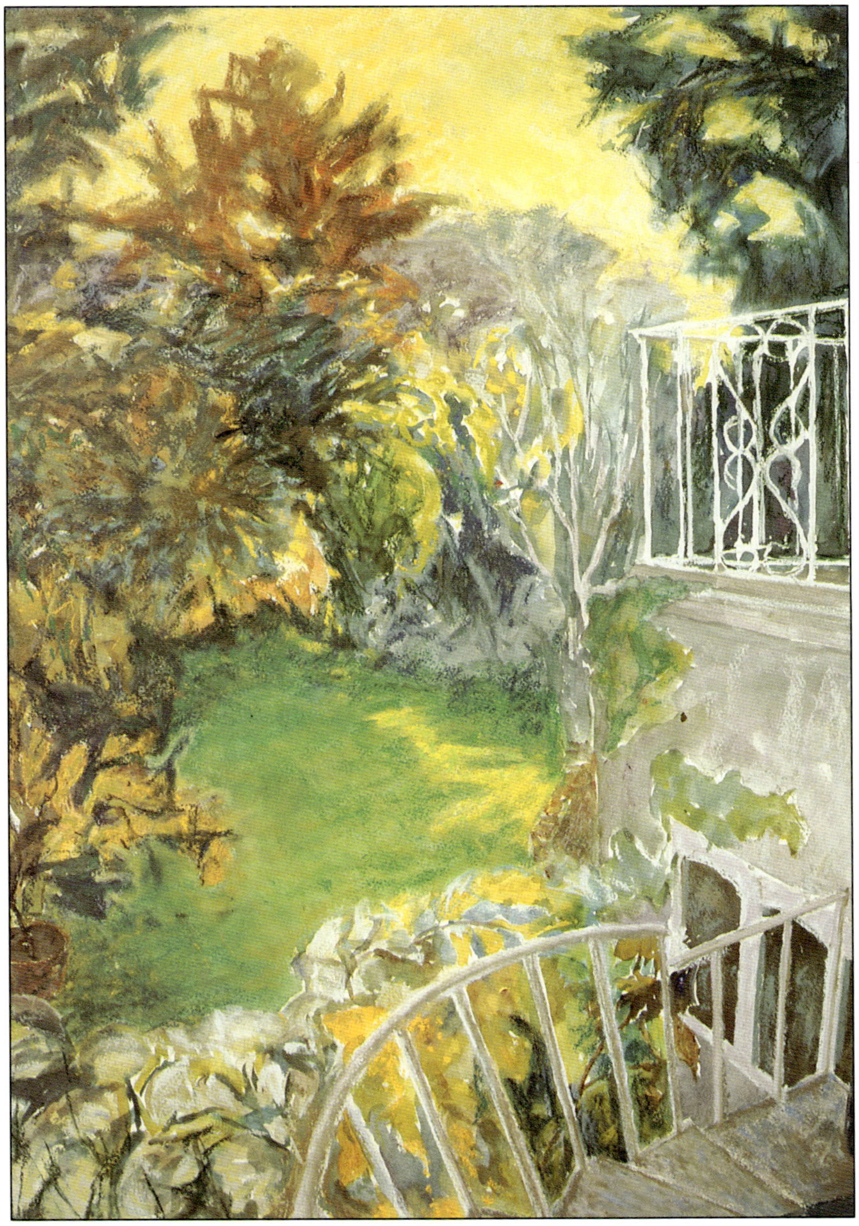

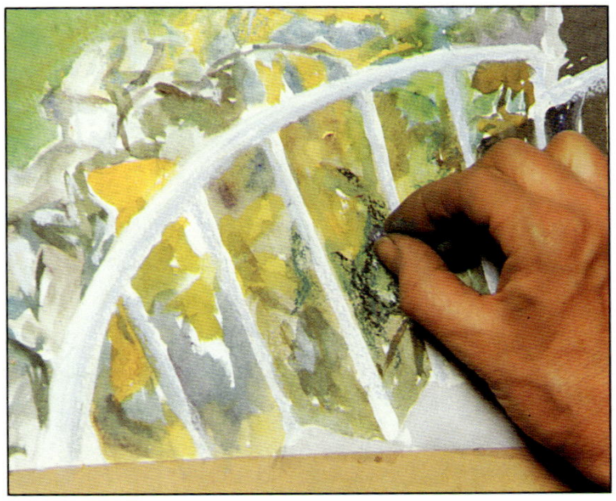

5 *The railings have been reserved as highlights, with the watercolour painted around them and later light applications of grey pastel giving a suggestion of modelling. The central area of foliage is now darkened so that the whites stand out clearly.*

6 (Above) *Some artists use a watercolour underpainting much as they would a coloured ground, covering most of it with pastel. In this case, however, the two media work together, with the watercolour playing an important part in the overall effect.*

Wet Brushing Oil Pastel

Oil pastel is an exciting medium to use, although it is very different in character from soft pastel, being bound with oil rather than gum. Its dense, rather greasy quality means that it fills the grain of the paper relatively quickly, making it less suitable for colour mixing by layering.

However, this is only true if the medium is used "dry" like conventional pastel. The great advantage of oil pastel is that the colour can be melted with an application of turpentine or white spirit and spread with a brush or rag over the paper (with canvas or oil-sketching paper as possible alternatives). This allows you to lay broad areas of colour very quickly and you can then work over these with more linear strokes, building up the picture with a succession of wet and dry layers. If the paper becomes clogged, you can remove whole areas of colour by applying more turpentine and rubbing gently with a rag. On oil-sketching paper you can make as many such corrections as you like, without harming the surface.

Oil pastels come in a more limited colour range than soft pastels, but this wet-brushing method allows you to achieve very subtle colour mixes on the working surface. As with paints, you can even mix colours on a palette before putting them on. Simply moisten the tip of a pastel stick with a brush dipped in turpentine to release the colour and transfer this to the palette.

As oil pastels are quick to use, easy to correct and, best of all, do not need fixing they make an ideal medium for outdoor sketching. However, they do have a tendency to melt under a hot sun, becoming very soft and buttery, which makes them hard to manage; it is best to work in the shade wherever possible.

Oil pastel and white spirit

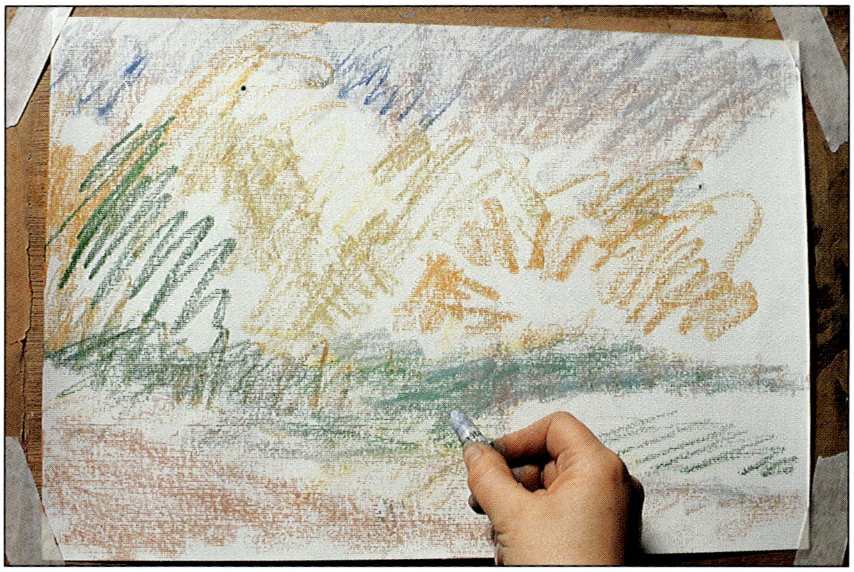

1 *Working on oil-sketching paper, the artist blocks in the composition lightly with very soft oil pastels. You can also work on ordinary pastel paper, such as Ingres, but there is a slight possibility of the oil in the pastels causing deterioration over time.*

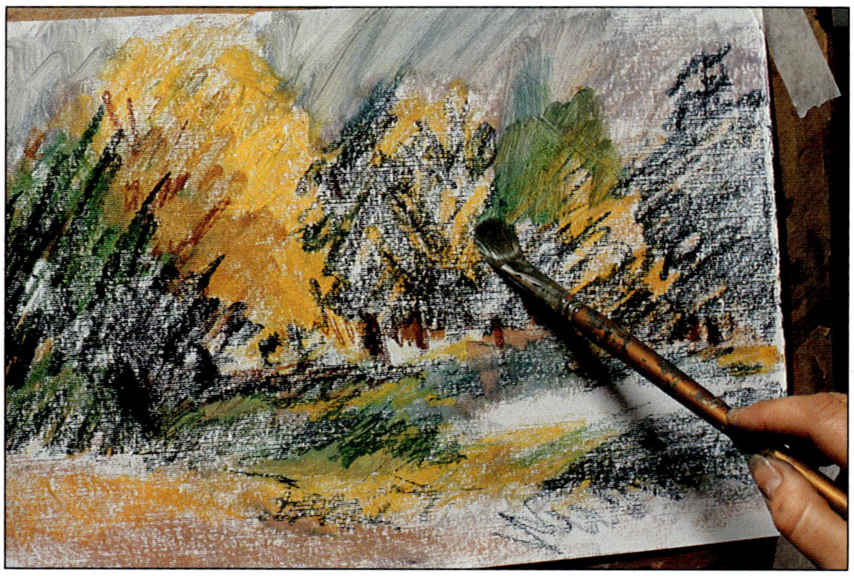

2 *A bristle brush dipped in white spirit is used to spread and mix the colours. The mixture is relatively transparent because the first colours were applied lightly. If colour is built up too thickly in the early stages, mixtures can become muddy and dull.*

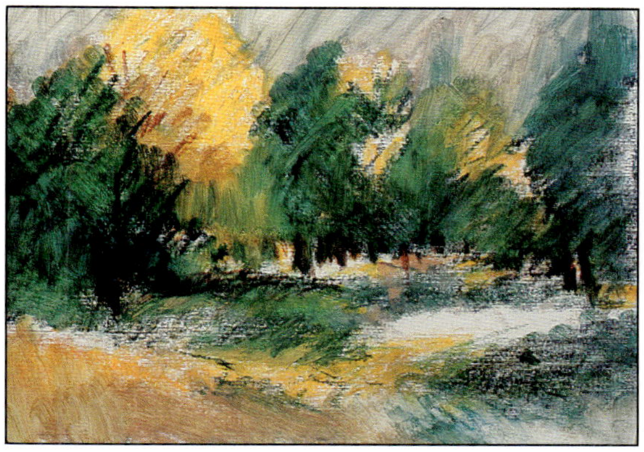

3 Further brushwork over the whole picture has now firmly established the form and colours of the trees. Again, you can see how the artist has avoided over-mixing and churning up the colours; blues and yellows can be clearly distinguished in the dark and light green areas.

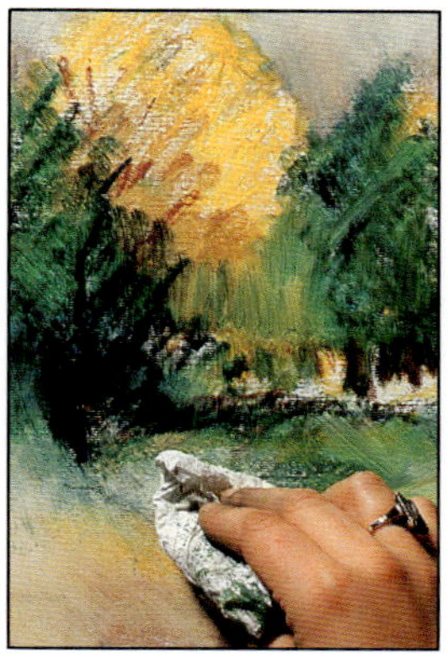

4 The beauty of this method is that amendments can be made simply by wiping off colour with a rag, dipped in white spirit. The foreground needs to be softened, so the whole area is wiped down prior to re-working.

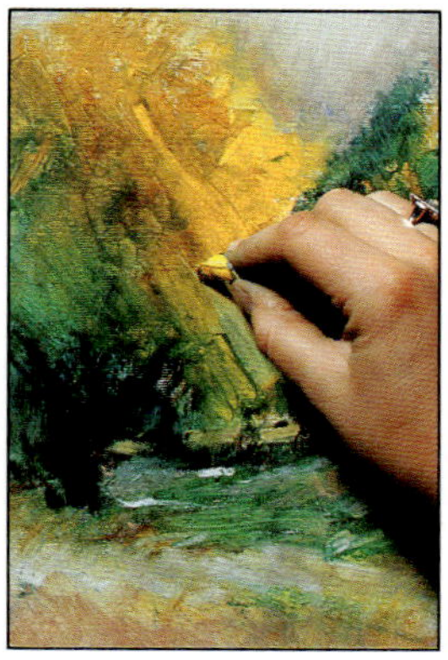

5 To produce a textured effect on the foliage, the artist works into a still-wet area with firm strokes of the pastel stick. This creates distinctive marks and slight ridges rather similar to the effects of sgraffito.

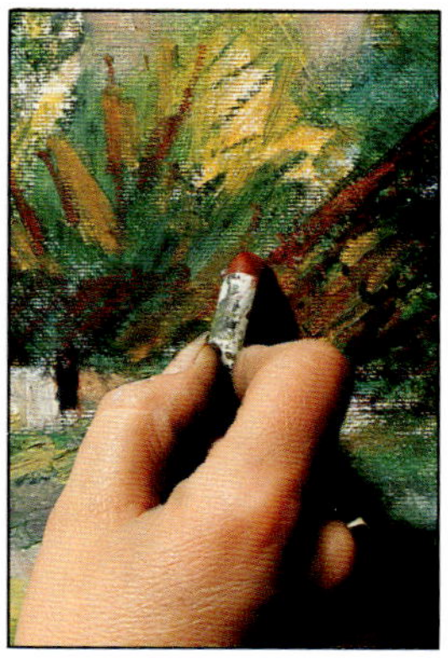

6 For colour contrast and a suggestion of the trunks and branches, dark red oil pastel is now used to draw over the earlier colours. The artist keeps the marks very broad and free; her approach is impressionistic.

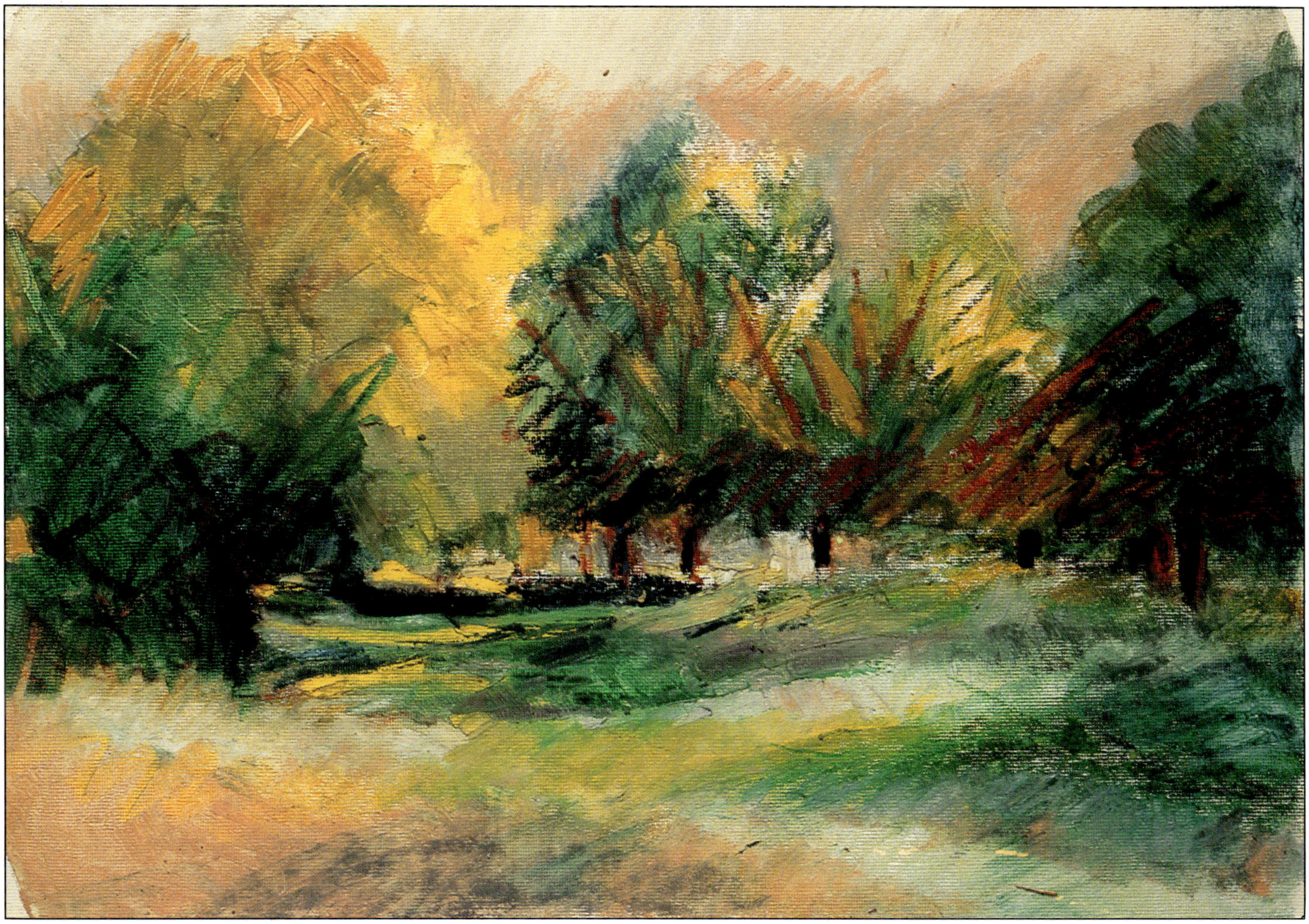

7 As the pastel has been used in a series of thin washes, rather like glazing in oil painting, the colours are beautifully luminous, an effect enhanced by the white paper reflecting through the colours. When using oil pastel in this way, white paper can be a better choice than coloured.

CHARCOAL AND PASTEL

Charcoal and pastel are frequently used together; they are natural partners because both have a similar texture. As underdrawings for pastel work should never be done in pencil – the greasiness of graphite repels the pastel colour – charcoal is often used to make the preliminary line drawing. Any loose dust is then brushed away and the charcoal is fixed before the pastel colour is applied on top.

In this case the charcoal is largely obliterated by the overlaid colours and plays no part in the finished work. However, it can also be used in a more positive way, with the charcoal complementing the pastel colour. As charcoal gives a clearer, crisper line than soft pastel, it is sometimes used to define detail and provide a linear structure, with the pastel used for the broader colour areas (like line and wash in watercolour painting).

Another approach, sometimes used for figure work and portraiture, is to make a tonal underdrawing, using the side of the charcoal stick to establish light and dark areas. This is suitable only for paintings which are to be relatively "low-key" in colour, as, even when the charcoal is fixed, the pastel laid on top picks up a little of the black dust. This has the effect of muting the pastel colours, which can be very effective for certain subjects.

Charcoal can also be used hand in hand with pastel colours and, because it is less dense than black pastel, it is particularly useful for the subtle mid-toned colours which are often hard to mix successfully. The grey-greens or grey-blues seen in the middle distance of a landscape, for example, can often be achieved by mixing charcoal and green or blue pastel, or by dragging a light veil of charcoal over a pastel colour to tone it down.

Making a charcoal underdrawing

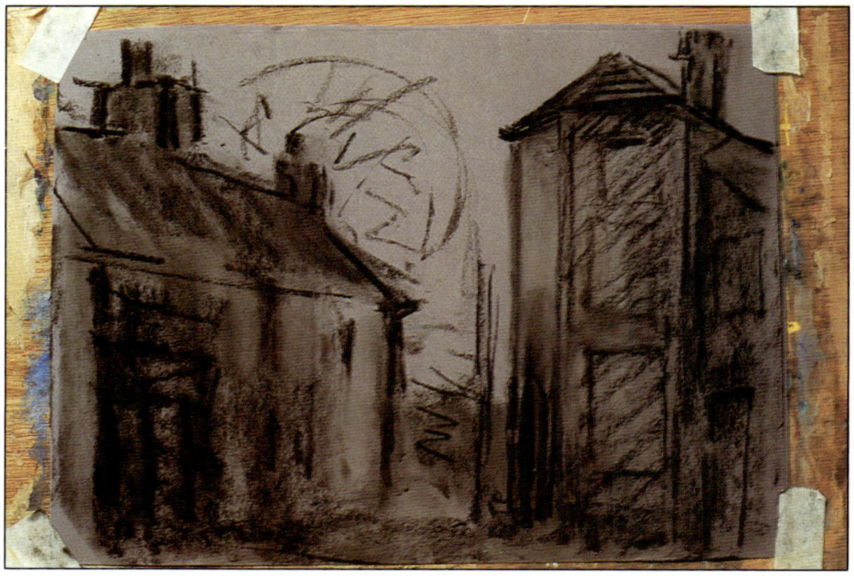

1 The colour scheme planned for this picture is relatively sombre, with a predominance of dark tones, so the charcoal drawing is made on a mauve-blue paper chosen to set the key for the later colours. The paper is Mi-Teintes, used on the smoother side.

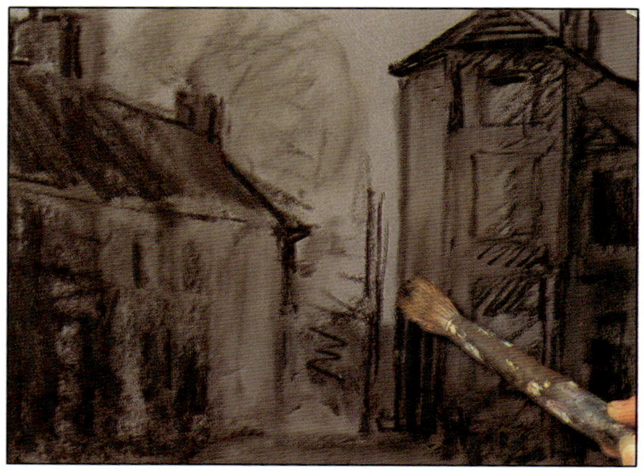

2 With the underdrawing complete, the excess charcoal dust is flicked off the paper with a bristle brush. The drawing is sprayed with fixative before the pastel colours are applied, so that the charcoal does not muddy the colours.

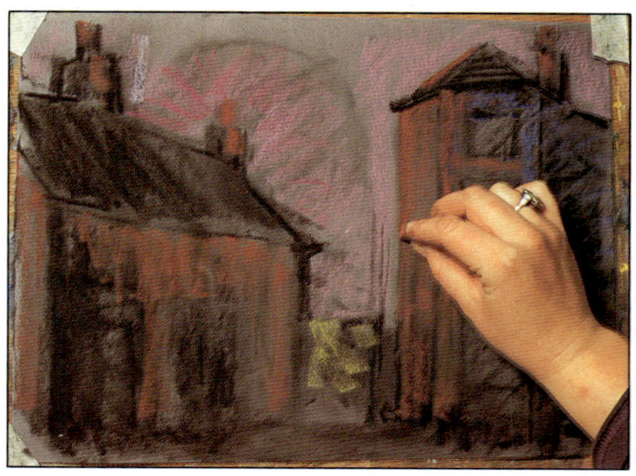

3 The artist's method is to build up her colours gradually with a series of overlays. The bright pink used for the sky at this stage will be modified by later applications. Although dark in tone, the colours chosen for the buildings are very rich.

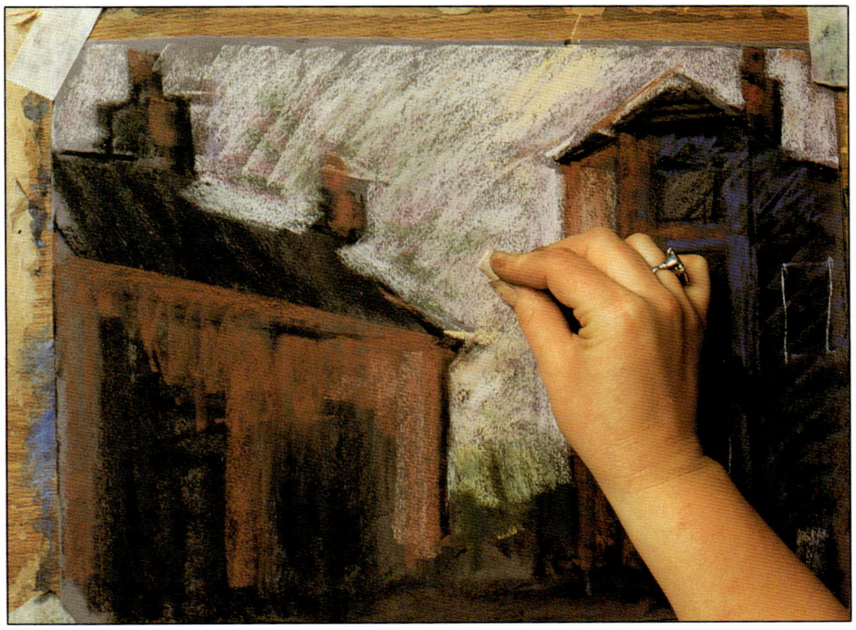

4 *The side of a short length of white pastel is now dragged lightly over the earlier pink; some of this is still visible, as is some of the paper colour. The sides of the buildings nearest to this sky area have also been lightened slightly.*

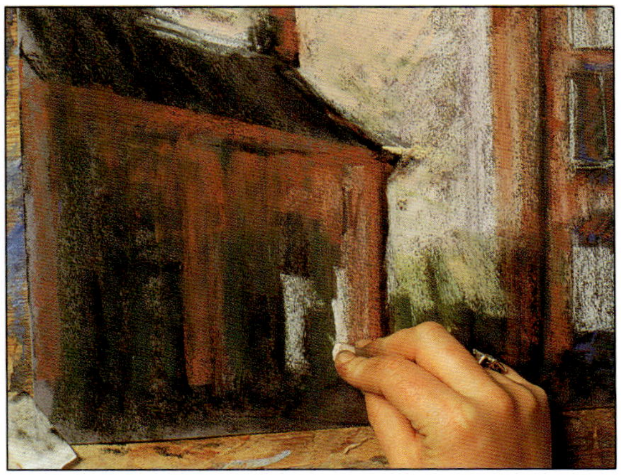

5 *The highlights have been left until the final stage, because pastels are opaque and it is therefore possible to cover dark colours with light ones. Notice the variety of colours used for the walls of the houses, from deep greens to reds and pinks, plus a mauve produced by the paper colour showing through the original charcoal drawing.*

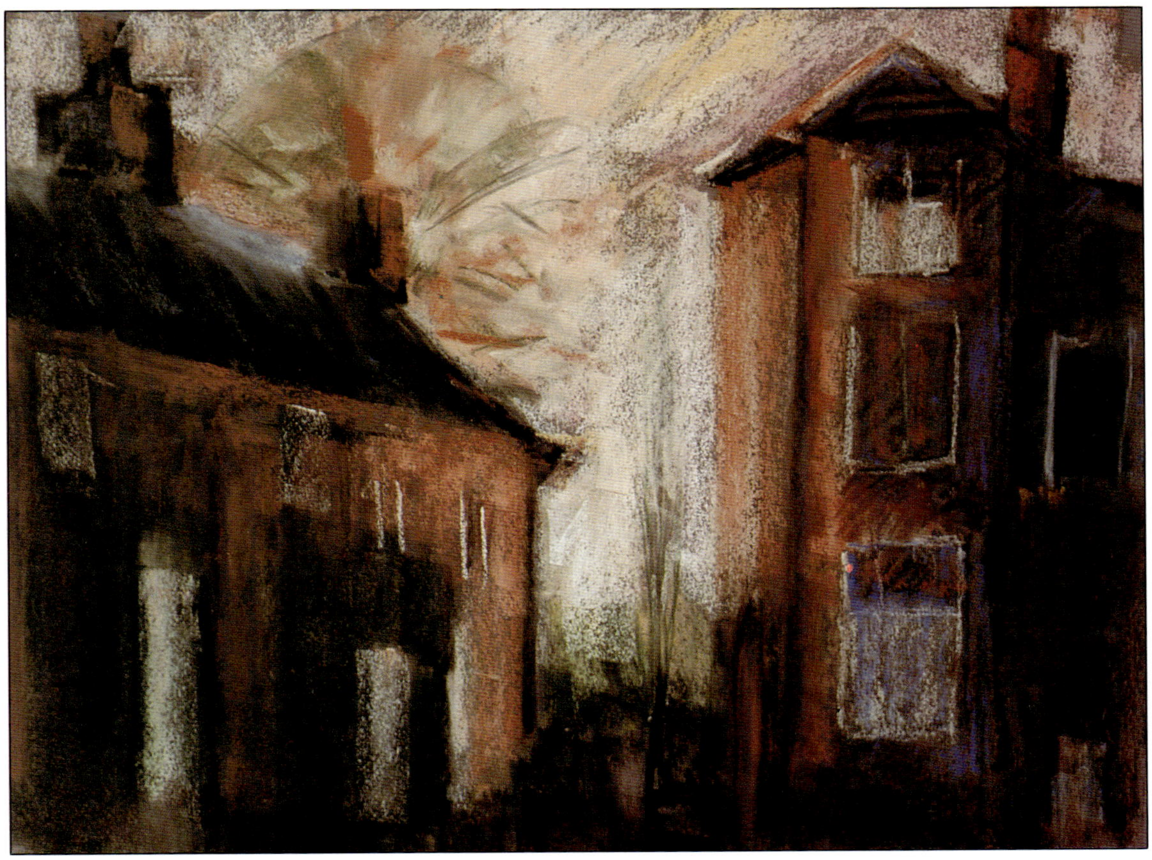

6 *Finishing touches have been added to define the details of the buildings with fine lines (made with the edge of a broken pastel stick), and to suggest the large tree behind the houses on the left. Both of the trees are important to the composition, but play a minor part, so they have been treated lightly, with smeared strokes, to merge them partially into the sky.*

Building Up Pastel

Although the standard pastel papers are versatile and allow for a certain amount of layering, you cannot build up colours really thickly on them. For those who like truly painterly effects, it is worth trying one of the special papers produced for pastel painting: sandpaper, velour paper and Sansfix paper.

These papers handle very differently from the normal pastel paper. Sandpaper in particular grips the pastel pigment so firmly that it is virtually impossible to blend colours by spreading them with either your fingers or a rag; for the same reason you cannot move colours around on the surface. However, the paper's firm hold on the pastel pigment means that you can go on layering colours more or less indefinitely. This creates very subtle mixtures and great depth of colour as well as effects similar to that of impasto in oil painting, where the brushstrokes stand proud of the surface. In fact, some pastel paintings on sandpaper look very much like oil paintings.

These papers all have one disadvantage: they are very "greedy" with the pastel colours and you will get through your pastels at a faster rate than when working on Ingres or Mi-Teintes paper. This is partially balanced by the fact that you won't need much – if any – fixative, which is fairly expensive. If you find the paper beginning to clog you can use fixative, but it is not normally necessary. It is best not to fix the finished painting, as this will tend to darken the colours.

Working on Sansfix paper

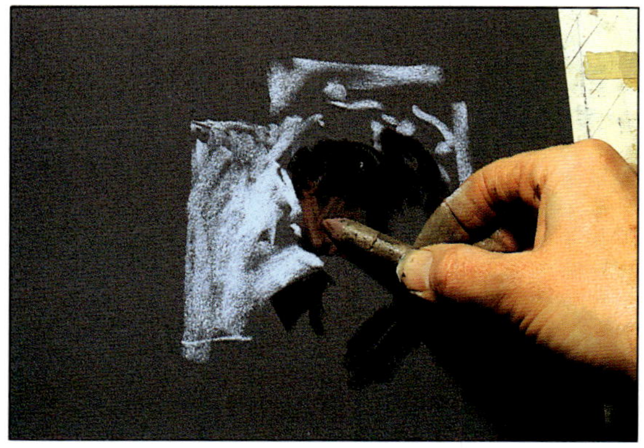

1 This paper grips the colour more firmly than the standard papers and is ideal for creating painterly effects in pastel. Here, the artist begins work on the lightest areas.

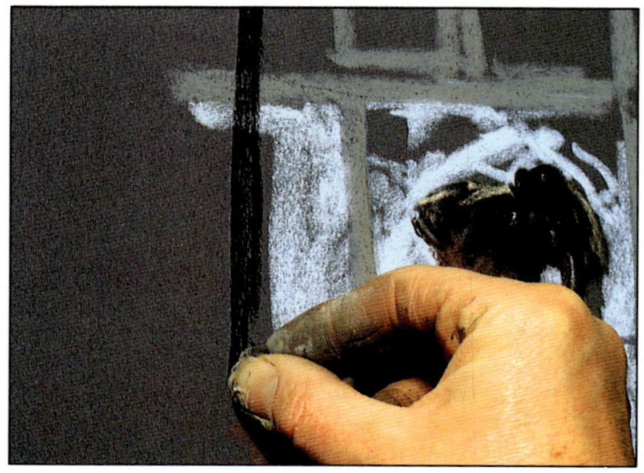

2 A solid line of black is now pulled down the paper to define the pole leaning against the windowsill, which provides a visual balance for the artist's easel.

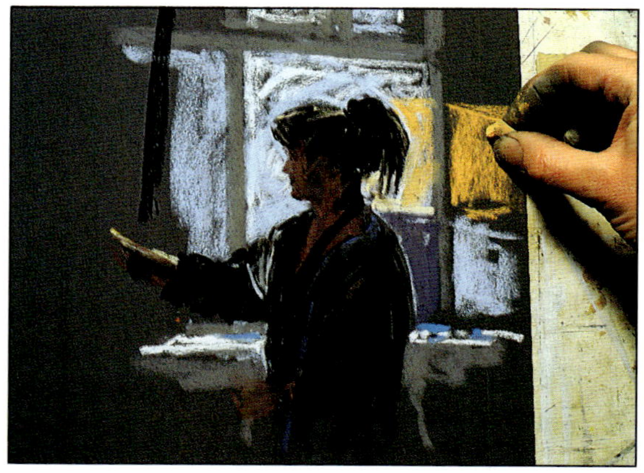

3 The colours on the face and body have been built up more thickly, and both grey and yellow added to the original application of white on the window. The paper allows for a considerable amount of building up by such layering methods.

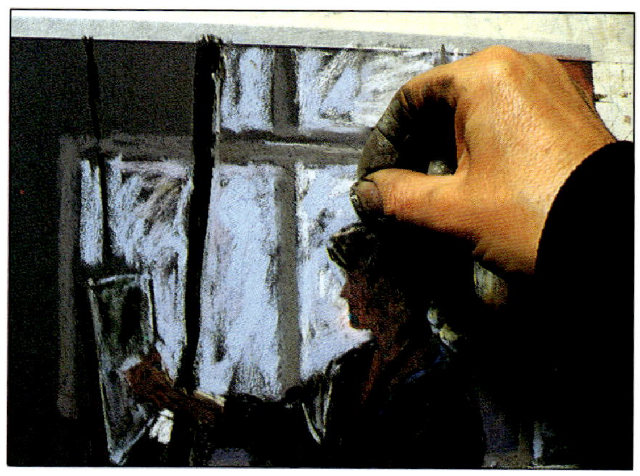

4 Using a small piece of pastel, the artist now lays light grey over the white. He has deliberately allowed small patches of the dark grey paper to show through to create a lively broken-colour effect.

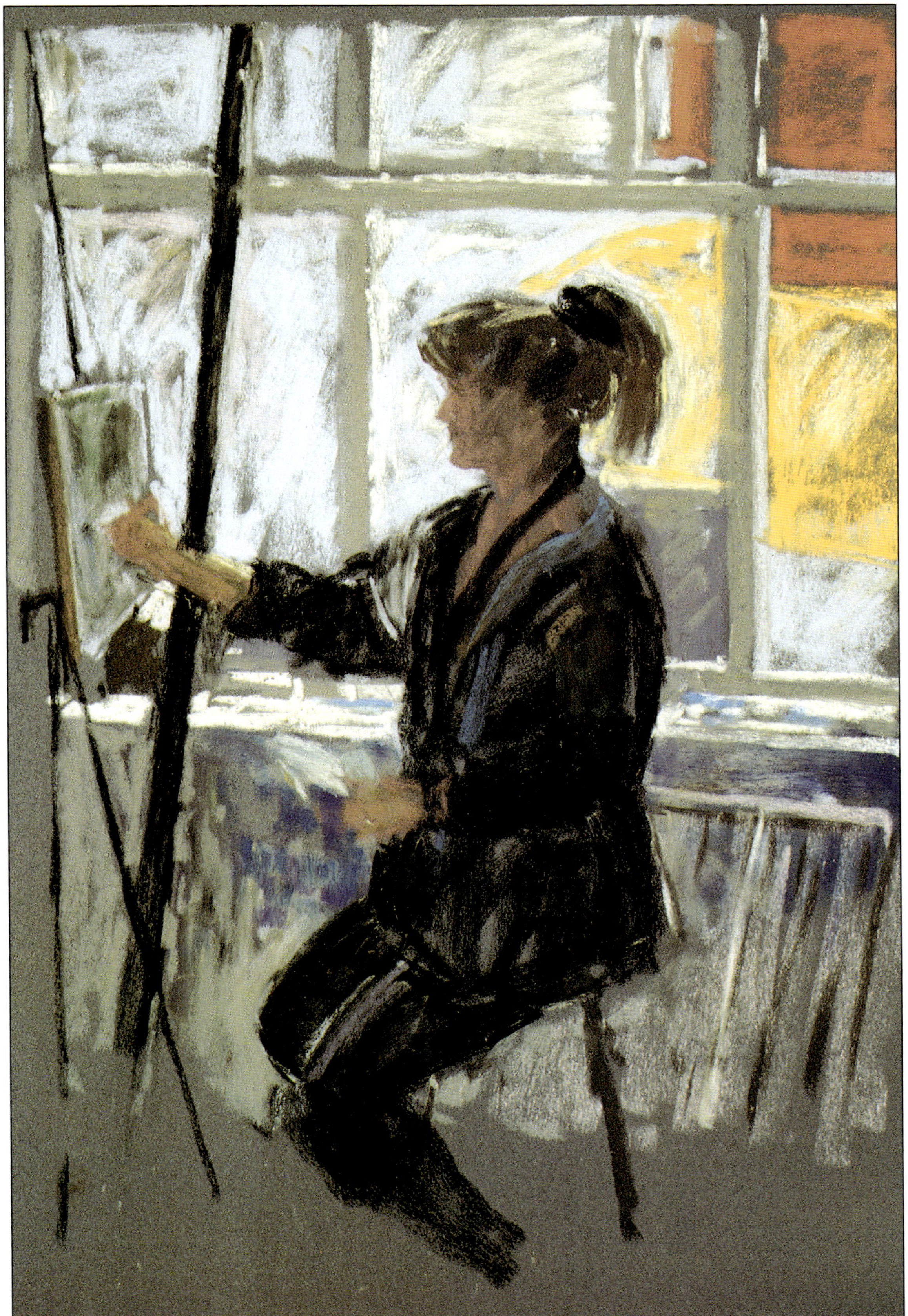

5 The finished picture, with its thick and heavy pastel marks, is reminiscent of an oil painting. This paper is not suited to very delicate approaches or to blending techniques.

Laying a Textured Ground

The underlying texture of the paper is always an important factor in pastel paintings. Some artists like to work on a texture of their own making, rather than relying on the mechanically produced overall texture of the paper. A "home-made" texture can take any form you like, but the most usual one is a series of irregular diagonal or vertical brushstrokes, which give a directional emphasis to the overlaid pastel strokes. Such grounds can be laid with acrylic paint, used fairly thickly so that it holds the marks of the brush, with acrylic gesso, or, for a really heavy texture, with a substance called acrylic modelling paste, thinned with water. The latter is only sold in large pots, however, and is quite costly, so make sure you like this way of working before you invest in it.

The advantage of using acrylic paint is that you can colour the ground as well as texturing it. You can even combine the texture element with a coloured under-painting, varying the colours and textures from one area of the painting to another. Don't overdo it, however, as you don't want to introduce too many different elements before you even begin to apply the pastel. This method is best suited to thick applications of pastel; you will need to work on a tough paper, such as heavy watercolour paper – don't try to lay a ground on ordinary pastel paper, as it will buckle under the weight of the paint.

A tinted and textured ground

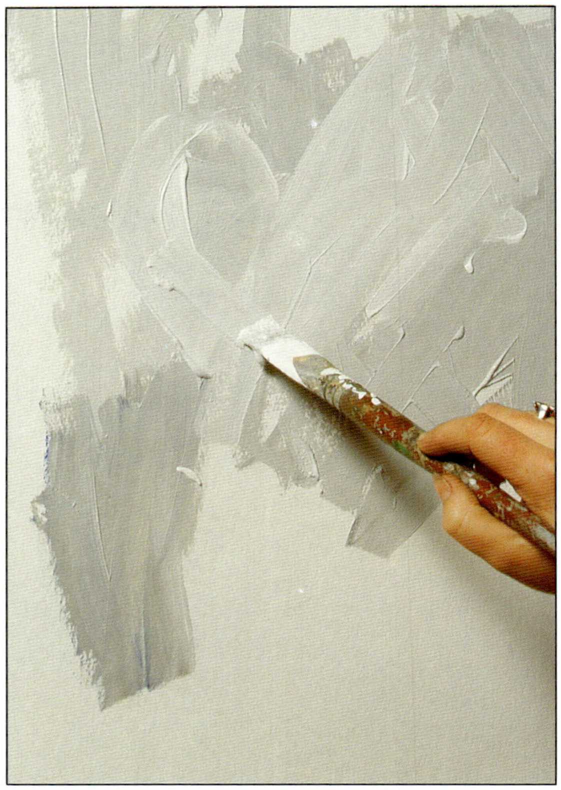

1 *Acrylic gesso, which is sold primarily for preparing boards and canvases for oil and acrylic painting, makes an excellent textured ground for pastel work. It is slightly thicker in consistency than tube acrylic and it dries fast. Here it has been mixed with black acrylic paint and applied to thick watercolour paper with a large bristle brush.*

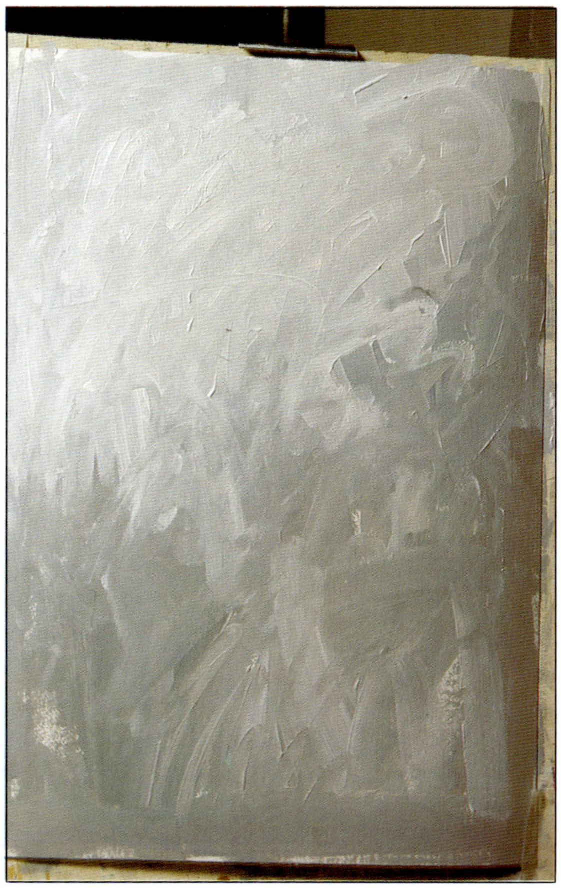

2 *The deliberately uneven application of the ground creates a surface which will break up the pastel strokes in interesting ways. This gives an exciting element of unpredictability, allowing you to exploit semi-accidental effects.*

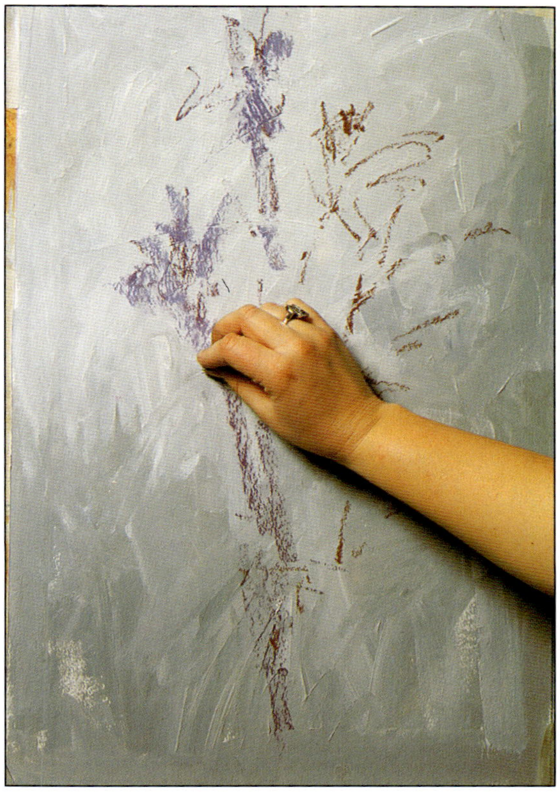

3 *As colour is scribbled over the brushstrokes of acrylic gesso, it catches only on the raised areas, creating a series of strongly textured marks. This is a method which is best suited to broad, impressionistic approaches; with a heavy underlying texture it is not possible to achieve fine detail.*

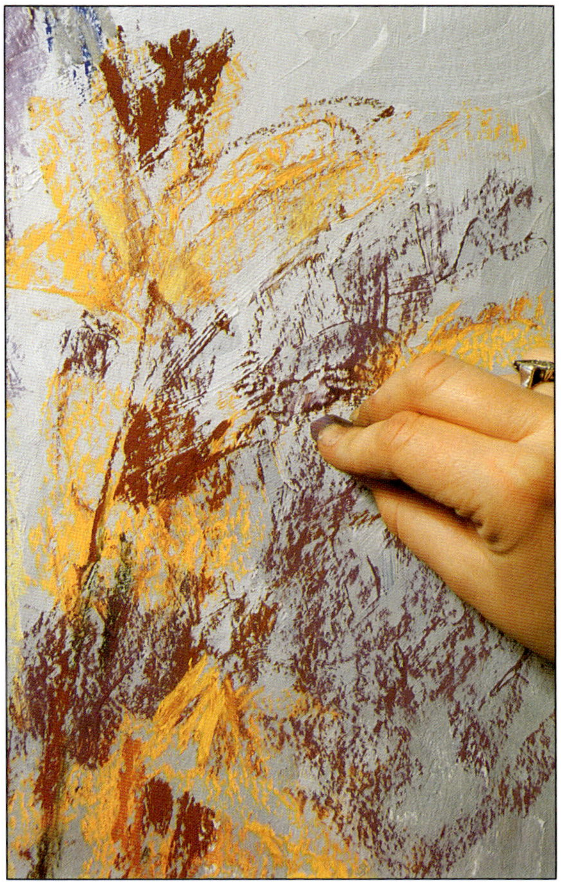

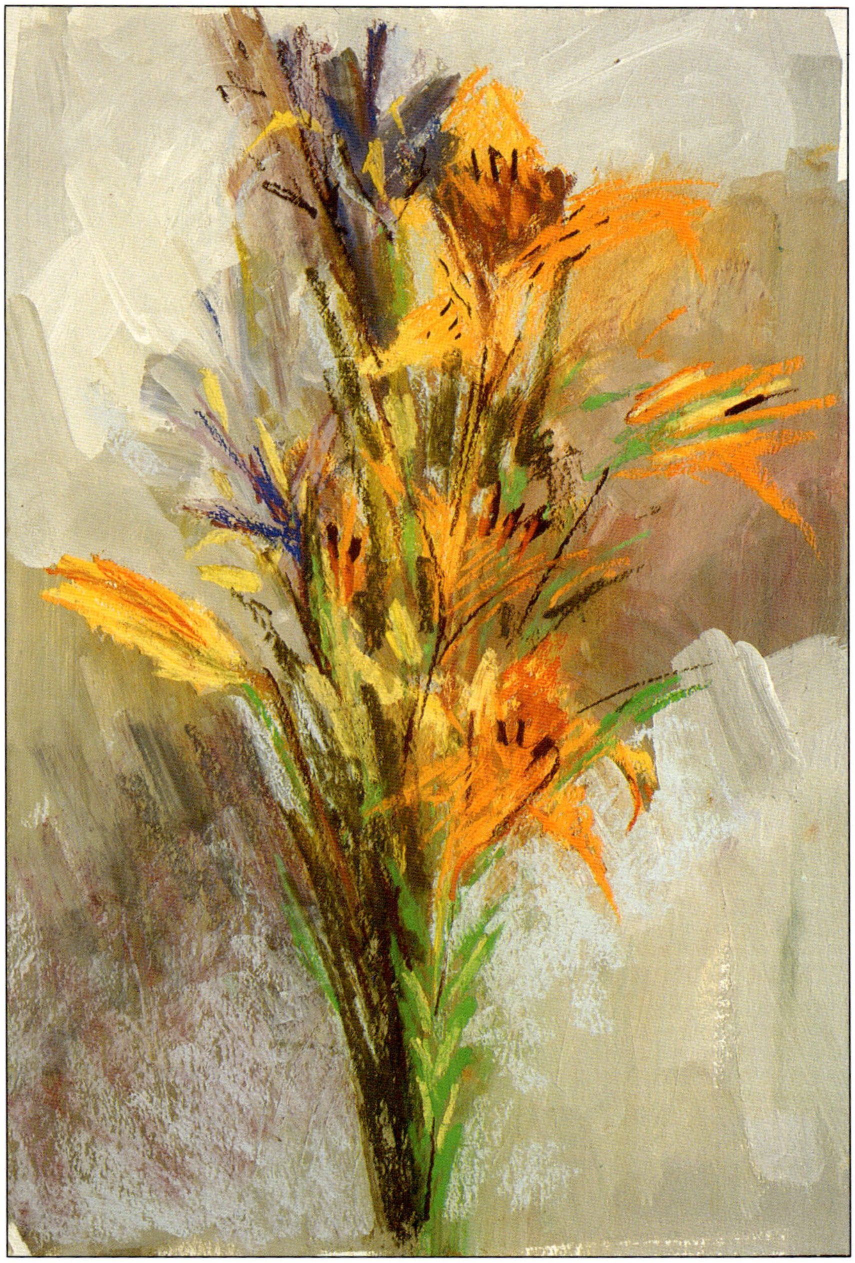

4 (Left) *Here the artist uses broad strokes of pastel to capture the essential colours and shapes of the flowers.*

5 (Above) *As the pastel cannot completely cover the brushmarks of the gesso ground, in the final stages the artist turned to a painting method, dipping a brush into gesso and painting over the pastel. This mixed with and spread the colour, giving a broad painterly effect.*

SGRAFFITO

This technique, in which one layer of colour is scratched or scraped into to reveal another one below, is sometimes used in oil painting. It is now also one of the recognized techniques in oil pastel, which is really oil paint in solid form. You can scratch into soft pastel, too, provided that you work on a tough surface, such as watercolour paper, and spray the first layer of colour with fixative before applying the second.

However, the effects are more dramatic and exciting in oil pastel and, because oil pastel colours cling to the surface very firmly and do not need fixing, they are tailor-made for the method. The effects that you can achieve are many and various, depending on the tool you use for the scratching, the amount of pressure you apply, the thickness of the colours and the texture of the painting surface. For example, if you work on a fairly smooth paper which doesn't break up the pastel strokes, lay one colour thickly over another and then scratch into the top layer with a sharp point, you can make a fine, delicate line drawing. Working on a more heavily textured paper and scratching into a layer of colour with the side of a knife, on the other hand, will give a broader, more generalized effect of broken colour, as the knife will remove only some of the colour. You can work either dark over light or light over dark, building up several different layers of colour then scratching into each one in turn; alternatively you can vary the colour combinations from one part of the picture to another – the possibilities of this technique are endless.

Sgraffito landscape

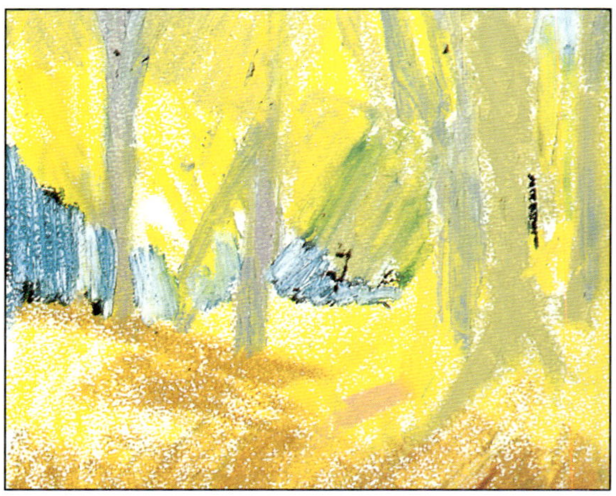

1 *Working on heavy watercolour paper, the artist has laid a foundation of light, bright colours which she will partially reveal by scratching back later colours with a knife or scalpel.*

2 (Right) *Dark greens, blues and red-browns have now been laid over the first colours, and a knife used to scratch into the central area and the tree at top left. To reinforce the broken-colour effect, much of the yellow has been left showing between strokes of green. This gives added vibrancy.*

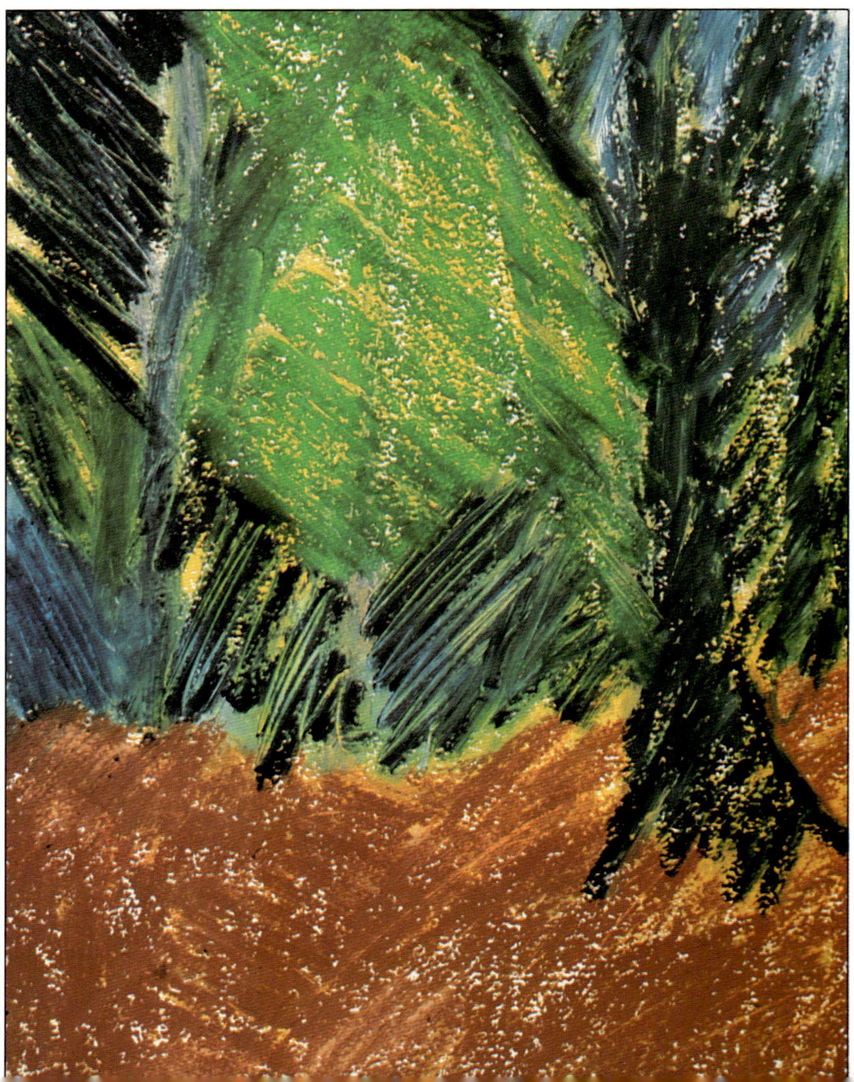

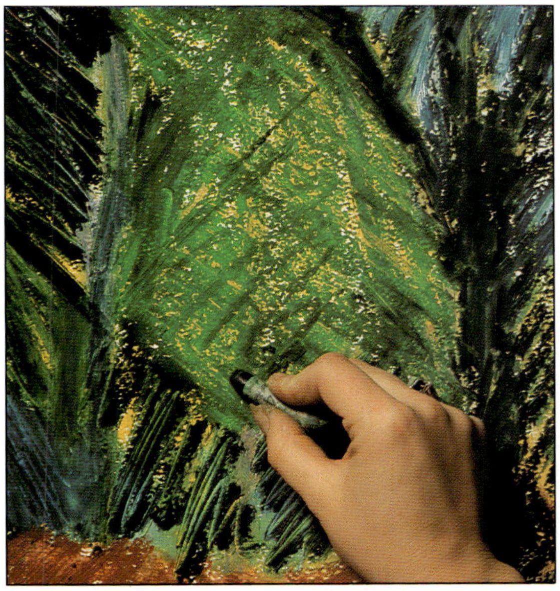

3 *Heavy diagonal strokes of deep blue are now laid over the green area in a loose cross-hatching technique. The pastel marks follow the same direction as the earlier scratch marks in order to integrate the sgraffito technique fully into the picture.*

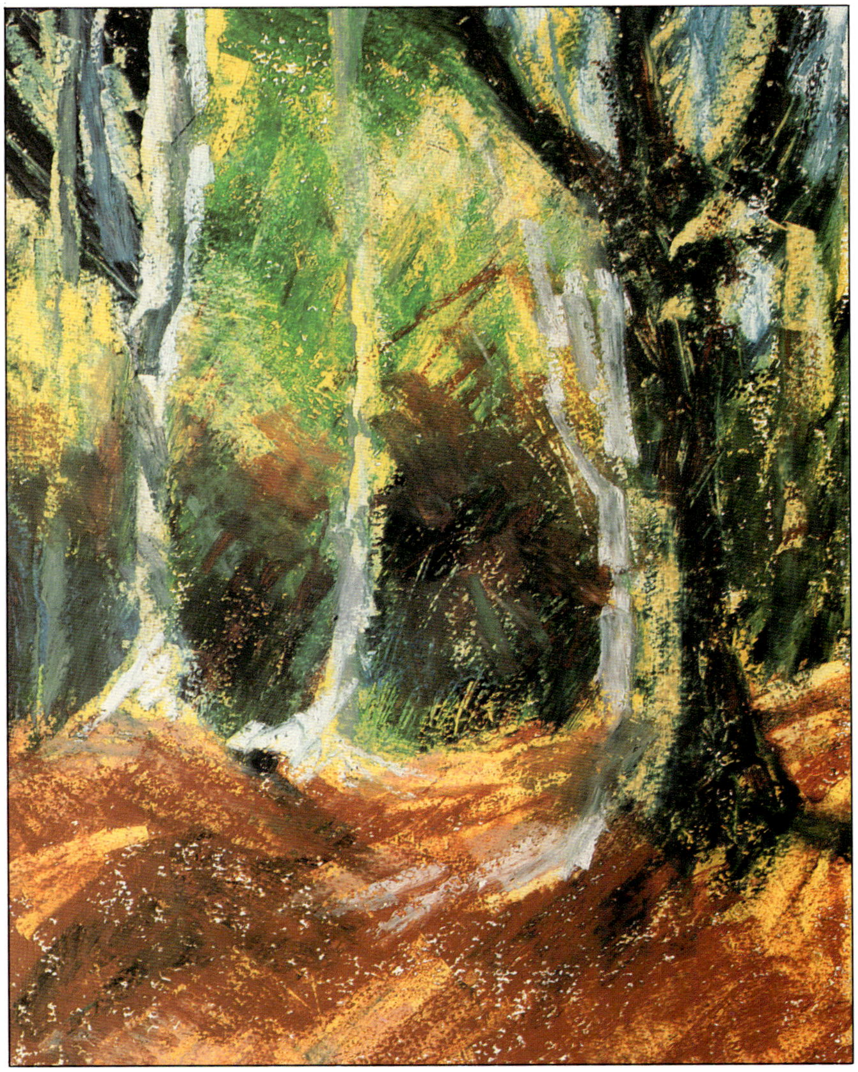

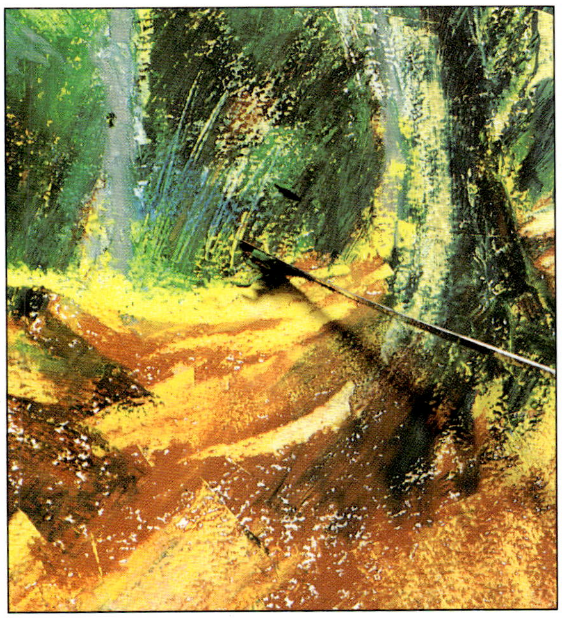

4 *With the point of a loosely held scalpel, the artist lightly scribbles into the layers of oil pastel. There is now a considerable build-up of different colours, and the scratching reveals brilliant blues and greens as well as the original yellow.*

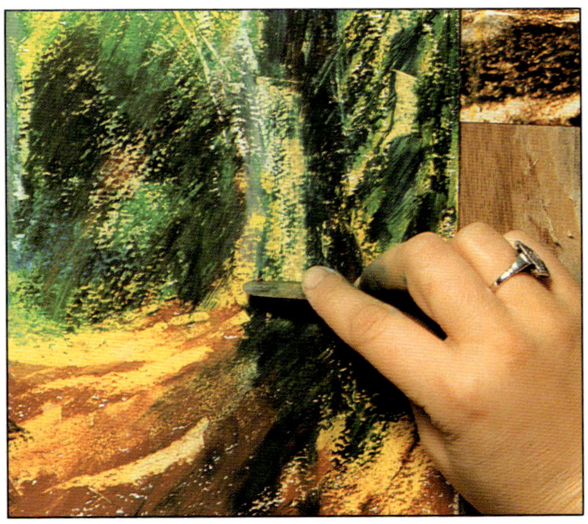

5 *Although the technique is most often associated with fine lines, broader effects can also be achieved; here, the side of a palette knife is pulled down the tree trunk. The palette knife has also been used to remove parts of the top colour in the foreground beneath the trees to suggest patches of strong sunlight filtering through the leaves.*

6 (Above) *The successive layers of scraped-back colour combined with the vigorous pastel marks create a lovely effect of shimmering light. The sgraffito has been carefully handled so that its effects are neither over-obtrusive nor self-conscious; this technique should never be allowed to dominate.*

COMPARATIVE DEMONSTRATION

If you visit an exhibition of pastel paintings you may well notice an amazing diversity of styles, even when the subject matter is similar. Three pastel landscapes by different artists, for instance, would probably bear little resemblance to each other, except in the medium used. Too often, amateur painters feel that there is a definite set of rules which must be followed, but, although hints can be given, there is really no right and wrong way of doing things. It is, instead, up to each person to develop their own methods and artistic "handwriting". To demonstrate this, we have asked three artists to paint the same simple subject. The first, Patrick Cullen, whose work is shown on these pages, paints on watercolour paper. Debra Manifold, the second artist, works in oil pastel on oil-sketching paper, while Hazel Harrison uses standard pastels and a more conventional surface – Mi-Teintes paper.

Pastel on watercolour paper

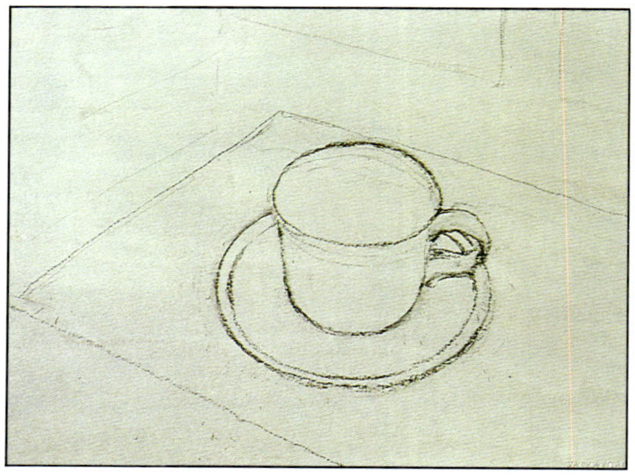

1 *The artist began by laying a light watercolour wash to tone down the white of the paper and make it easier to assess the first colours. When the wash was dry, he made a careful charcoal drawing.*

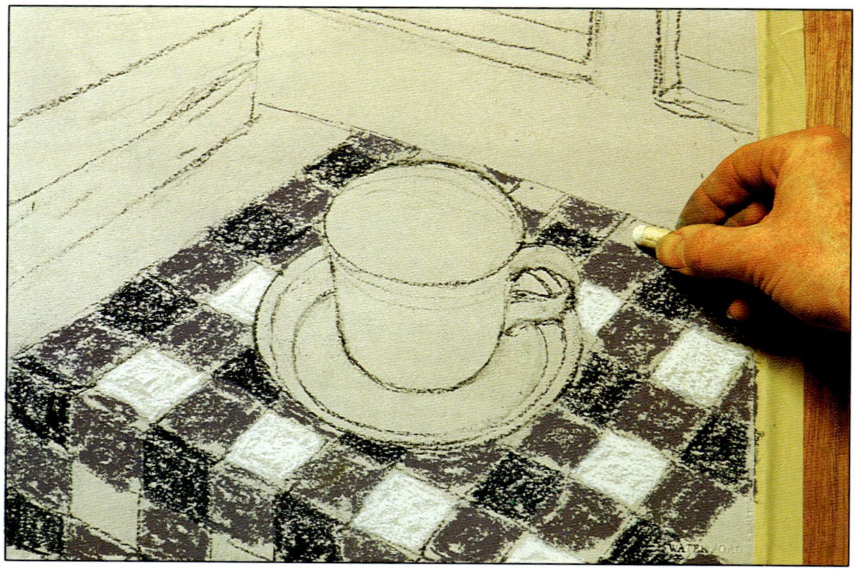

2 (Above right) *His method of working is unusual: instead of laying down broad areas of colour at the outset and modifying them later, he proceeds methodically across the picture, treating each area separately. He is now completing the tablecloth, which will provide a context for the other colours.*

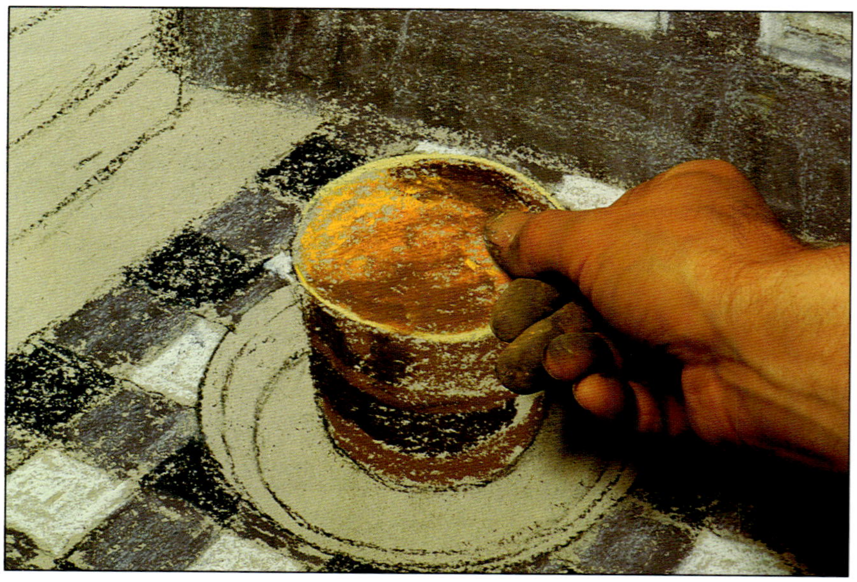

3 (Right) *To link the tablecloth to the bottom of the windowframe, which was painted next, the same grey was used. The cup and saucer provide the warmest colour area; the artist begins work here by defining the ellipse at the top and then blending the colours with his thumb.*

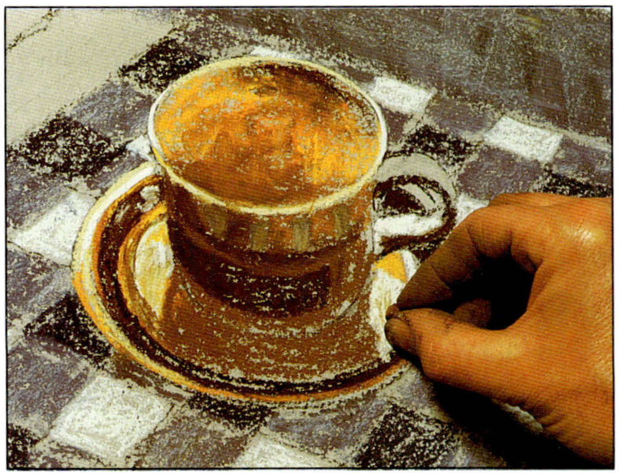

4 *The highlights on the saucer, like the ellipse on the top of the cup, define its shape, so they have been drawn in firmly in white. Few highlights are pure white, however, so they are now modified with light strokes of brown laid on top.*

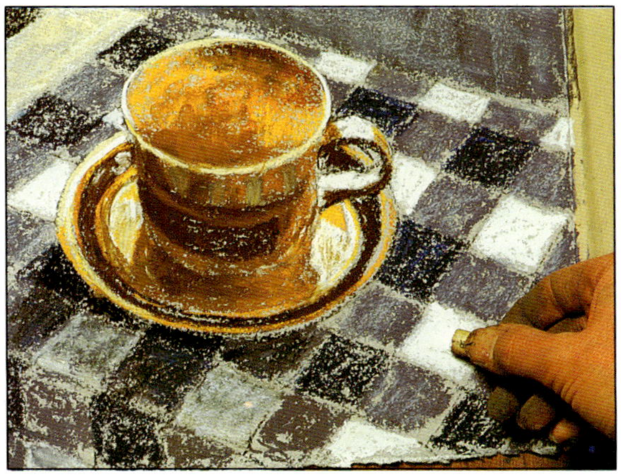

5 *Although the tablecloth was more or less complete in the earlier stages, there was insufficient contrast between the shadowed area below the cup and this right-hand side where the light falls. This is now lightened with pure white.*

6 (Below) *In spite of the simplicity of the subject and the limited colour scheme, the picture is satisfying and well-balanced, with the dark shapes of the window and the boxes on the left making a frame for the cup and saucer.*

Continued ▷

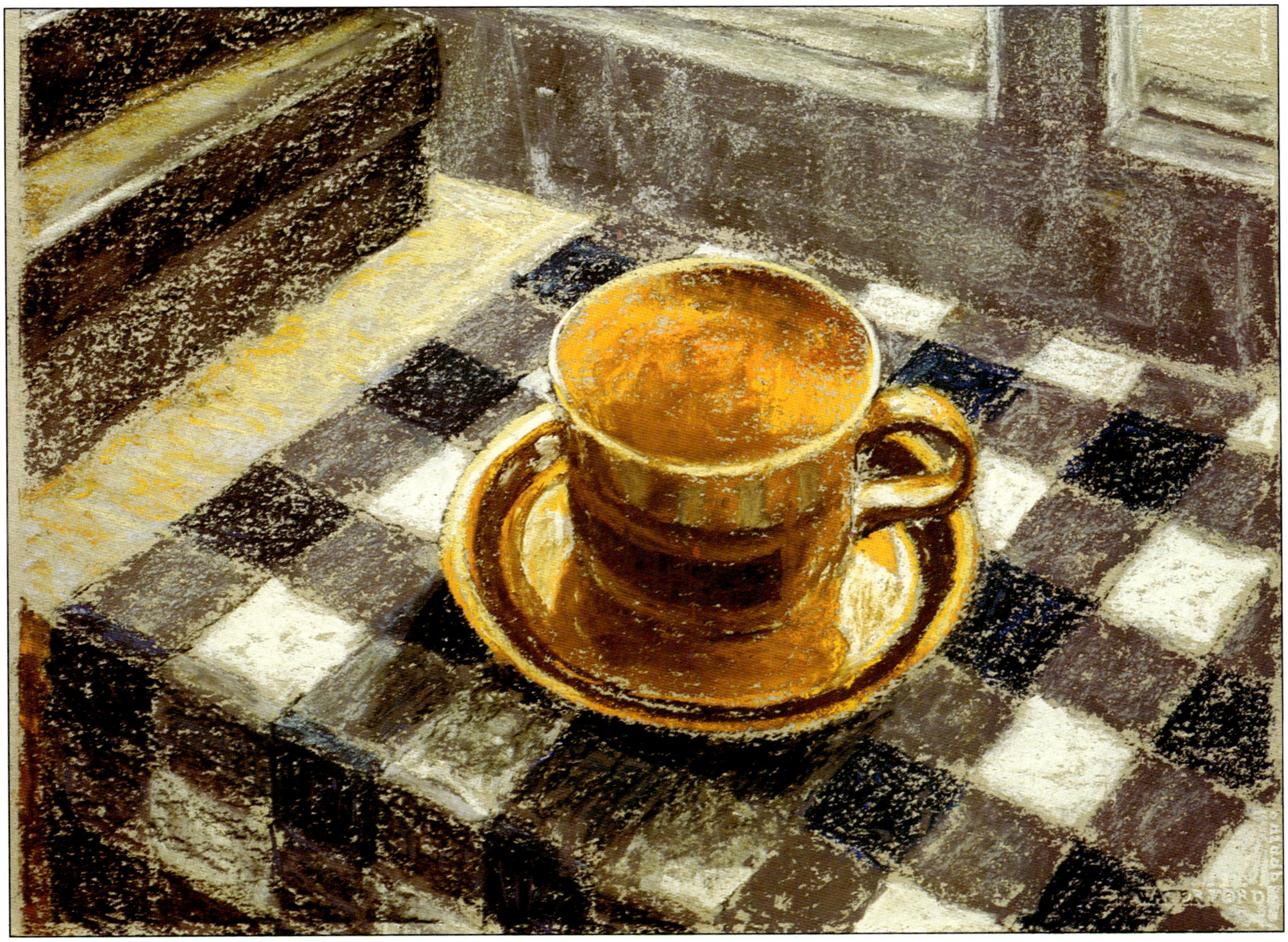

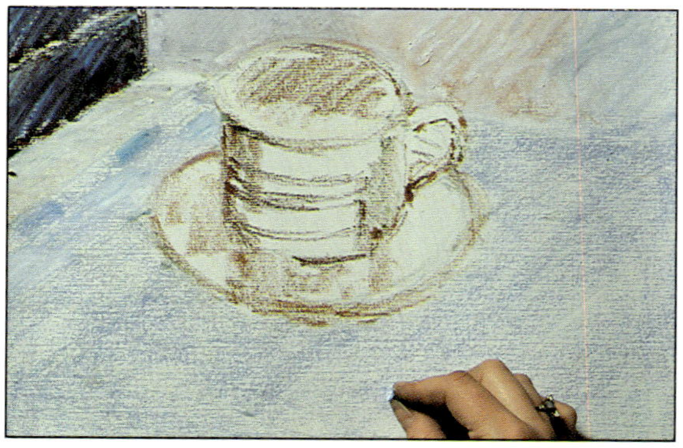

2 (Right) *The colours have been built up, and a brush dipped in white spirit is used to blend them. In order to balance the warm pinks and browns of the cup, similar colours have been introduced into the background.*

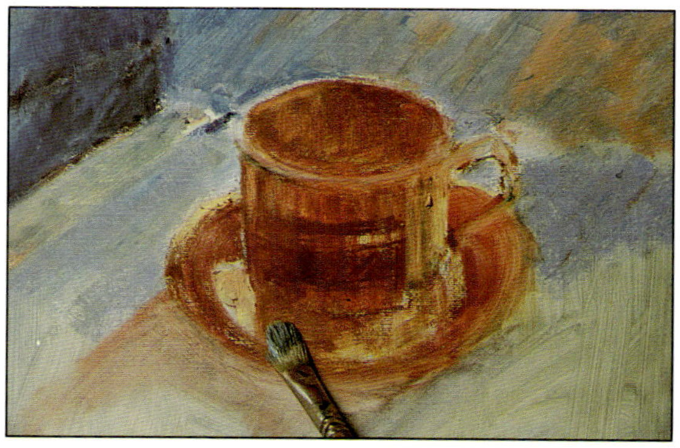

1 (Above) *The artist begins with a rough drawing in grey oil pastel and then applies light veils of colour with the side of the stick. Her drawing need not be as detailed as that of the previous artist because oil pastel can so easily be corrected.*

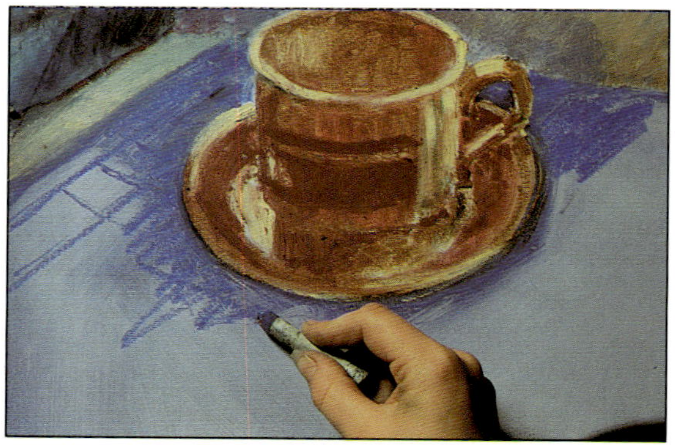

3 *This artist is always more concerned with the colour relationships in her painting than with the actual colours of the subject; here she chooses a vivid blue to contrast with the cup and saucer.*

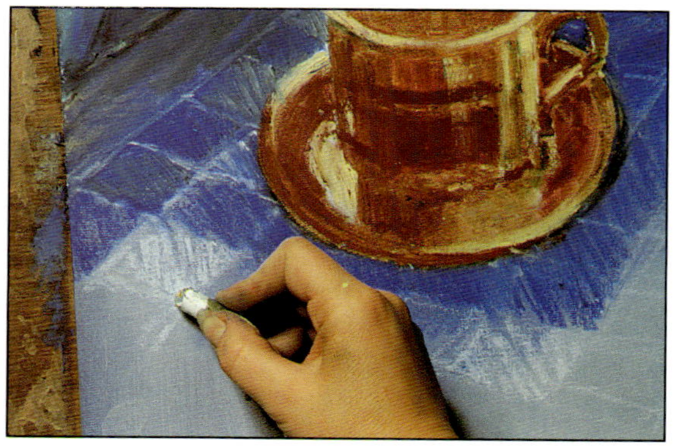

4 *Having mapped out the grid of squares for the tablecloth, she now scribbles white pastel lightly over the blue, using diagonal strokes which blur and soften the lines to avoid too precise an effect.*

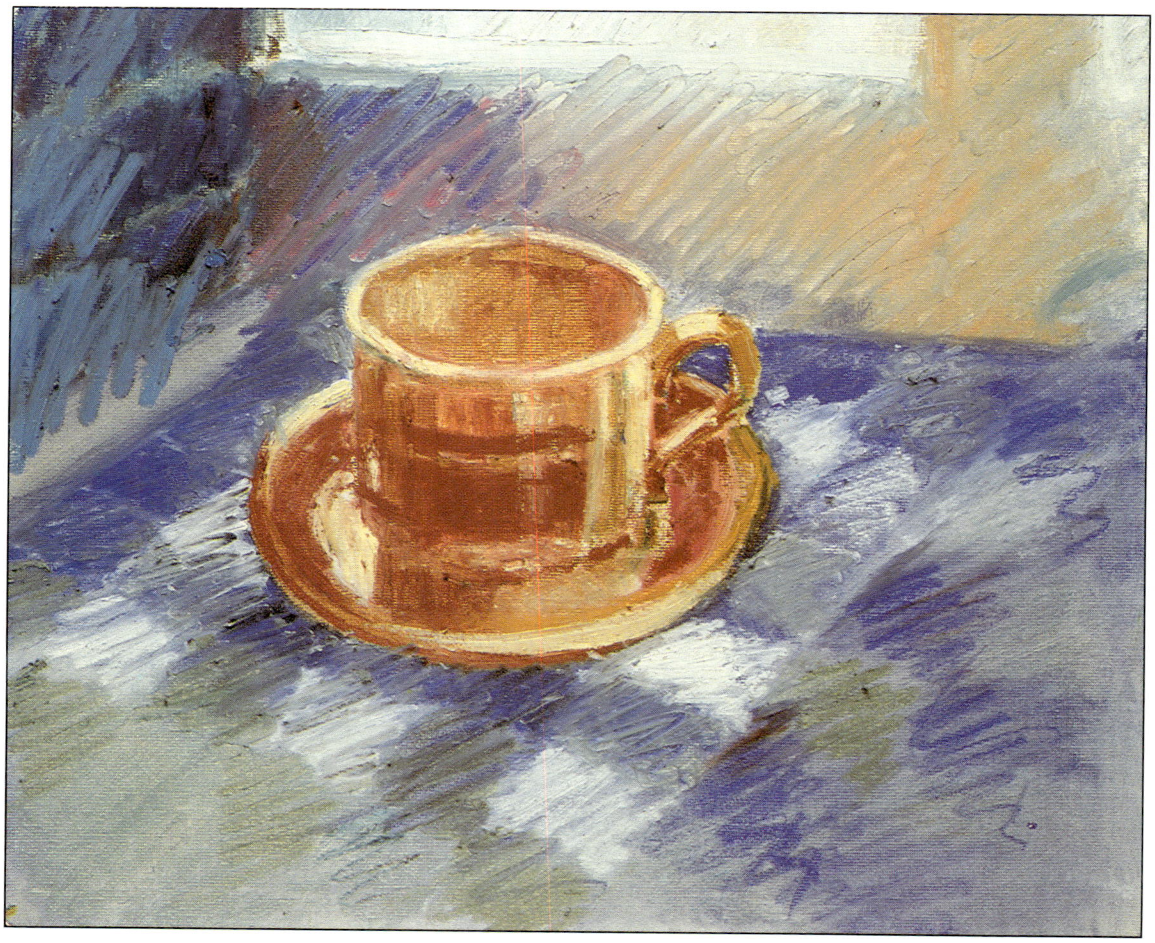

5 *The painting, with its vivid array of colours in the background and greenish blue in the foreground, is quite unlike the previous artist's interpretation. The style is very different too; the tablecloth has been treated in a much broader way and plays a less important role in the composition.*

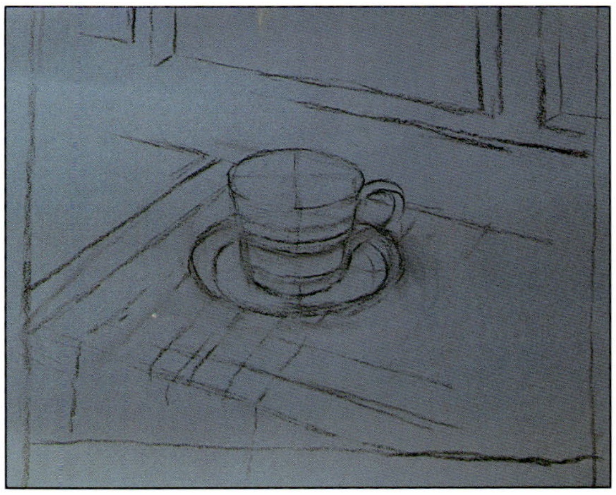

1 *A dark blue paper has been chosen to pick up the colour of the tablecloth. Working on the smooth side, the artist has begun with a charcoal drawing.*

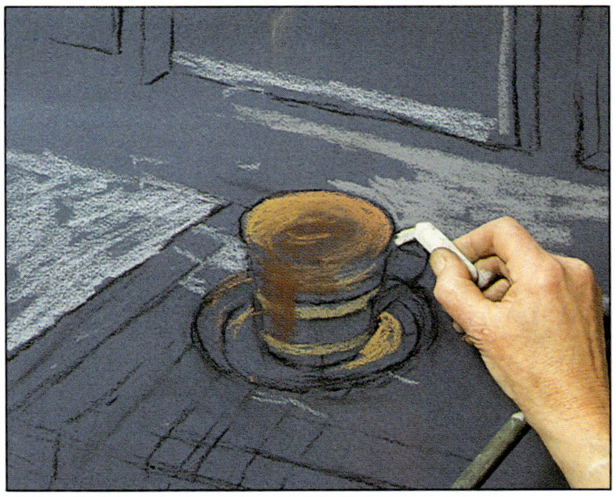

2 *The cup and saucer are seen as the key colour area, so she concentrates on this, finding it easier to assess the colours in the subject when working on a contrasting paper.*

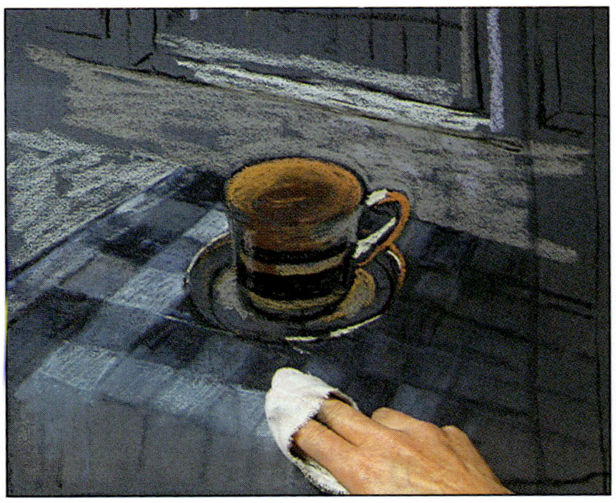

3 *At this stage it becomes apparent that the perspective of the tablecloth is wrong, so the whole area is wiped down with a rag. Pastel cannot be erased completely, but removing the loose pigment makes it possible to over-work.*

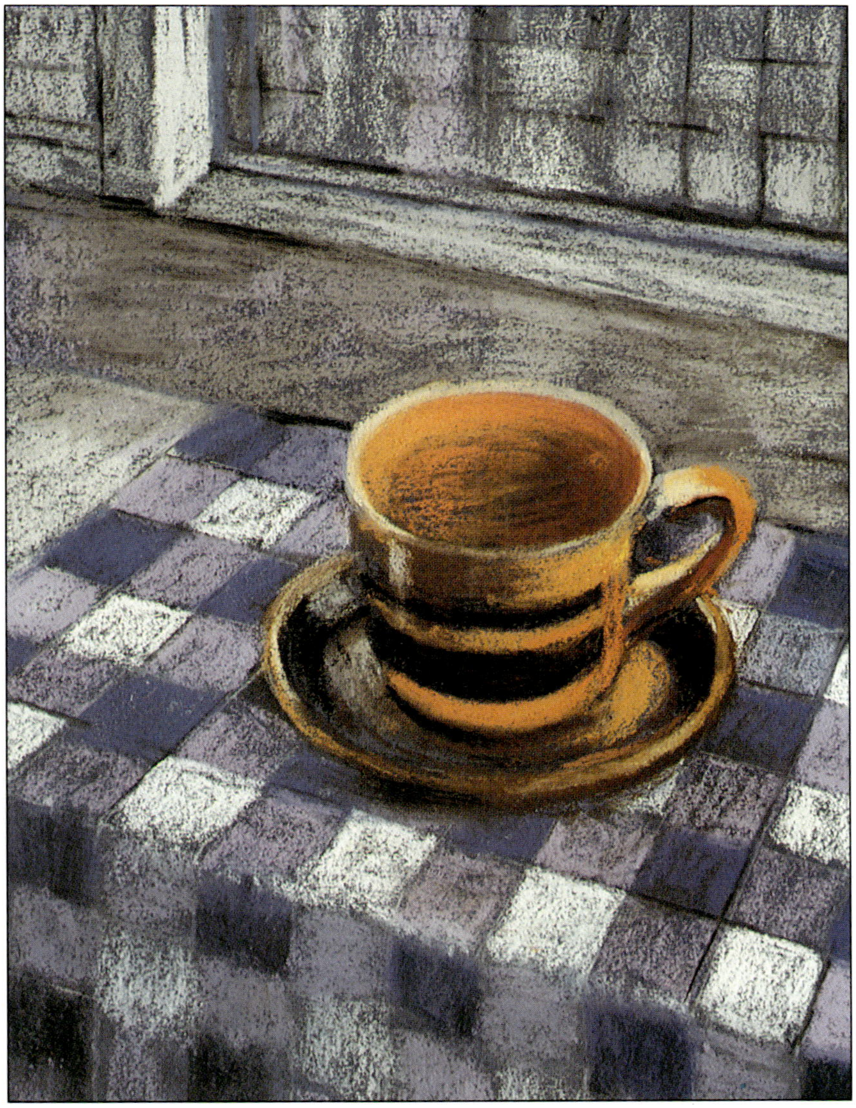

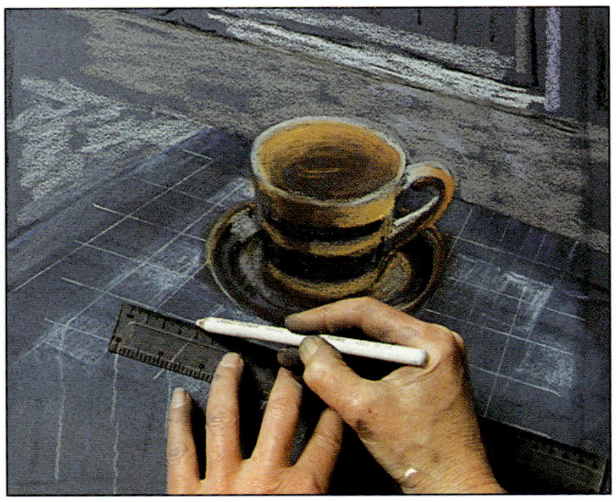

4 *A ruler and white pastel pencil are now used to re-draw the grid of squares. Straight lines are not easy to draw, and rulers can save a lot of frustration.*

5 (Above) *The artist changes the composition from a horizontal to a vertical format by placing masking tape around the central area. The ellipse of the cup is then re-defined with white pastel. Finally, the artist lightly sketches a grid of squares on the window to echo the tablecloth and introduces some touches of mauve-blue into the background.*

Focus

LANDSCAPE

Both soft pastels and oil pastels are ideal for landscape work. The range of marks that you can make – from soft blends and sweeping strokes made with the side of the stick to sharp, linear marks – is capable of matching virtually any effect seen in nature. Both types of pastel are quick to use, allowing you to build up areas of colour very rapidly, and are perfect for capturing fleeting effects of weather and light.

Best of all, if you are working outside directly from the subject, you will need far less equipment than you would with paints. The only basic requirements are your box of pastels, some paper and a drawing board. However, there are one or two other items that you may find useful.

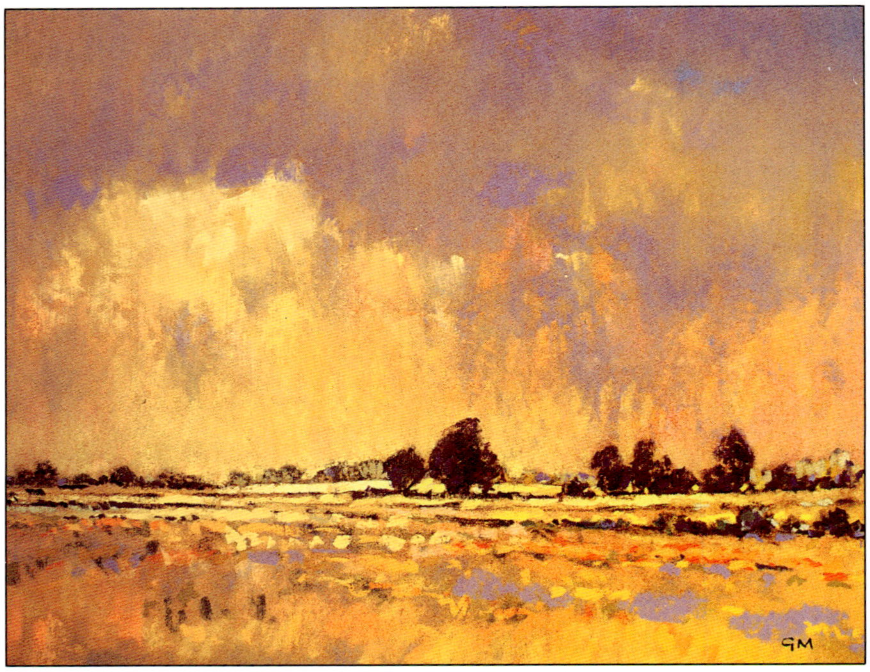

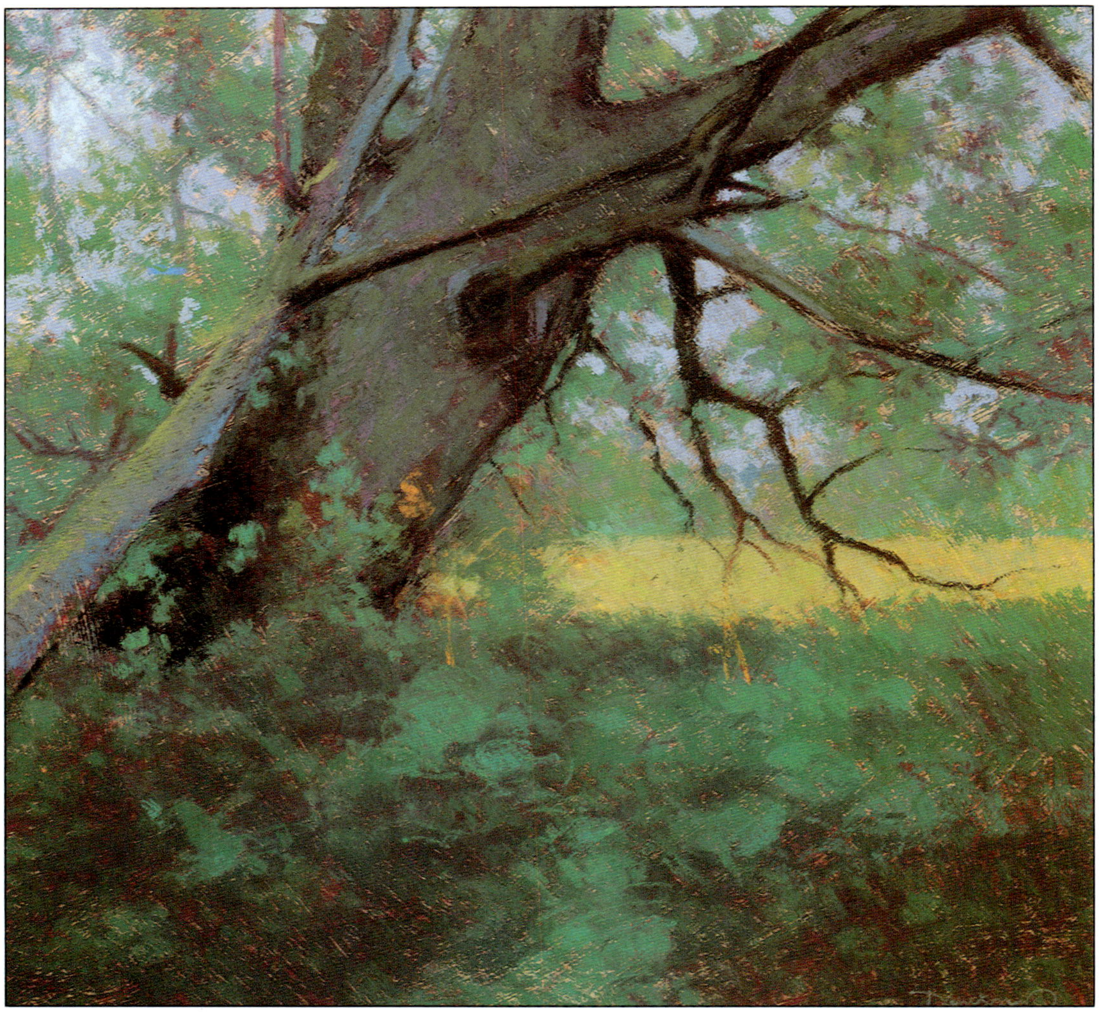

Landscape in close-up
(Left) *One of the most difficult decisions to make when faced with a large expanse of countryside is how much to include and what to focus on. You can often make a more expressive statement by moving in close, as Doug Dawson has done in* The Edge of the Meadow. *The strong diagonal thrust of the tree across the picture is balanced by the horizontal bands of colour formed by the foreground and by the light field in the middle distance.*

Tonal contrast
(Right) *A common cause of failure in landscape paintings is lack of attention to tones – the relative lightness and darkness of colours. In James Crittenden's* Spanish Landscape *the contrasts of tone not only convey the heat and strong sunlight, but also create a pattern of light and dark which gives a structure to the composition.*

Placing the horizon
(Opposite) *In a wide, panoramic landscape it is important to consider how to divide up the picture space, and how much prominence to give to the sky. The area of England in which Geoff Marsters works is very flat, with the great expanse of sky one of its most noticeable features, so in* Fen Landscape *he has given it three-quarters of the picture.*

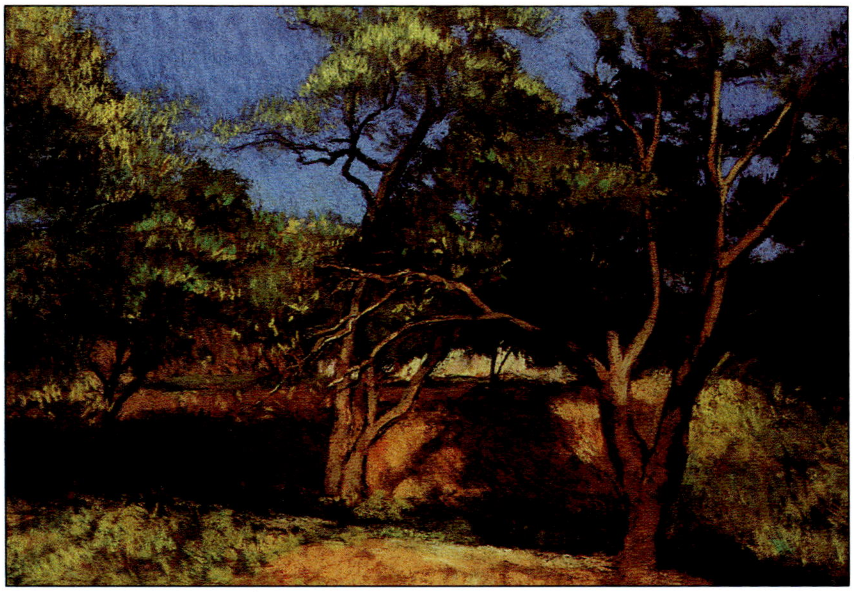

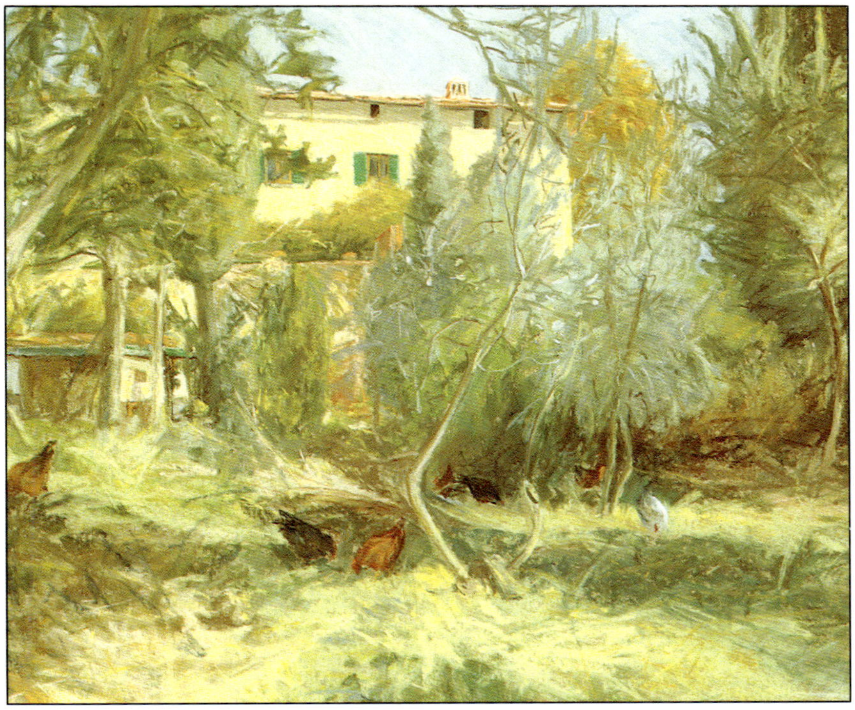

Varying the greens
(Above) *Landscapes are frequently spoiled by poor observation of colours, particularly greens. Greens are extraordinarily varied, and you must further take into account the many nuances caused by light and shade. In Patrick Cullen's* Chickens, Petrognano, *the "greens" vary from silver-greys and creamy yellows to near-browns.*

If you work on a large scale using soft pastel you may need to invest in a portable sketching easel. You will quickly be covered in pastel dust if you try to work with your board propped on your lap, and an additional advantage of an easel is that you can step back from your painting periodically to assess it.

You will get your hands dirty whether you use an easel or not, so take some rags or, better still, a packet of moistened hand wipes. For oil pastel you will need white spirit and rags to clean your hands, plus brushes if you intend to spread the colours. You will not need fixative for oil pastels but you will do for soft pastels, as it is easy to smudge unfixed, finished work when you are carrying it home.

Planning in advance

Even though time is usually limited when you are painting on the spot, it always pays to do some initial planning: choosing the best viewpoint, deciding how much of the scene in front of you to include in the picture and considering where to place the horizon. There is a natural tendency to divide the picture into two distinct areas of sky and land. This is not usually the best approach, however, particularly if it creates a central division – over-symmetry should always be avoided as it makes pictures look both dull and disjointed.

Give particular consideration to skies which are vitally important in landscape; not only are they the primary light source, they also play a major role in creating space. In a wide, panoramic landscape, for example, you can often increase the sense of depth and space by letting the sky occupy more of the picture area than the land – perhaps three-quarters of it. Conversely, with a mountain scene in which you want to express the upward thrust of the land, you could give minimum space to the sky.

Foregrounds are another important area – a painting can be easily spoiled by a weak or over-dominant foreground. As a general

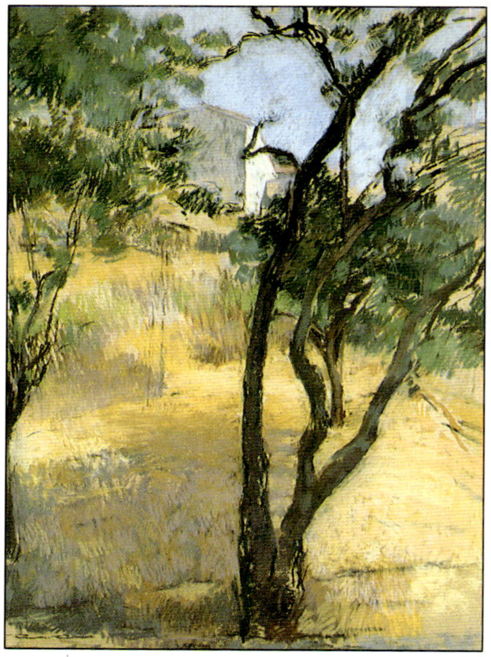

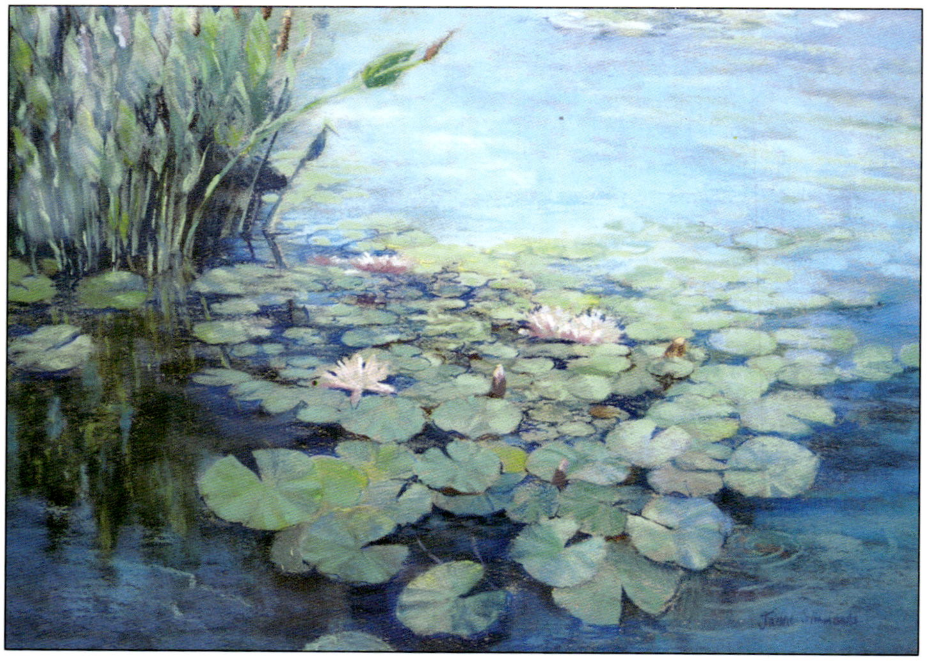

Mark-making
(Above) *The marks you make with your pastel sticks are as important as brushstrokes in an oil painting. As well as helping to describe the forms, they add an extra dimension to the picture, giving it a life and movement of its own independent of the subject it represents. In James Crittenden's* Looking through the Blue Trees, *short directional strokes play a practical role in describing the leaves of the trees, but even in the foreground shadow individual marks are visible, "lifting" an area which might have become dull if treated in a flat way.*

rule, foregrounds should "introduce" the rest of the picture and lead the eye into it. Too much detail or very strong shapes in the foreground can sometimes have the opposite effect, acting as a block, or a closed door rather than an open one. You can often solve the foreground problem in advance by choosing the best position from which to work – how much of the foreground you see is directly related to whether your viewpoint is high or low. If you look at a scene first standing and then sitting down, you will notice how it changes completely. In a flat landscape, particularly, some feature in the foreground which you may have scarcely noticed suddenly becomes dominant, while objects in the middle distance are diminished in importance. There is no reason why you should not choose a low viewpoint – for a subject such as mountains it could be ideal – but it is often better to stand at an easel to paint, or to find a vantage point such as a low wall.

Making changes

As pastels are opaque and one colour covers another quite easily, you can often change the composition in the early stages, perhaps by lowering a horizon or generally moving things around. However, it is a good idea to guard against possible failure by taking a larger piece of paper than you think you will need and letting the composition grow as you work. Leave generous margins around the edges so that you can expand the picture at the top, bottom or sides if you need to – this is one of the many advantages of painting in pastel.

You can also make changes to the composition afterwards by cropping, a device often used by photographers to work out which area of a negative to print. When you re-assess your work a day or two later indoors, you may feel that it is not entirely satisfactory, although you are not sure why. Usually it is a compositional problem: for example, you may have placed some feature too centrally or included too much sky. If you cut four "corners" of thick paper or cardboard and move them around on the picture, you will be able to visualize possible improvements. A small change such as taking an inch or two off the foreground on one side can change the whole feel of the picture and bring it to life. Some artists do not bother over-much about composition when they are working on location, but do it all afterwards by cropping. Don't actually cut the painting, though – just make a mount (matt) which covers the unwanted areas.

Painting water

(Opposite) *Water is one of the most attractive painting subjects, but it is not as easy to paint as it seems. Although many different colours and tones can be discerned, particularly in reflections, they must be carefully controlled. In Jackie Simmonds's* Waterlilies and Reeds *the strongest contrasts of tone are those between the lilies and the foreground water – a deep, rich blue reflected from the sky.*

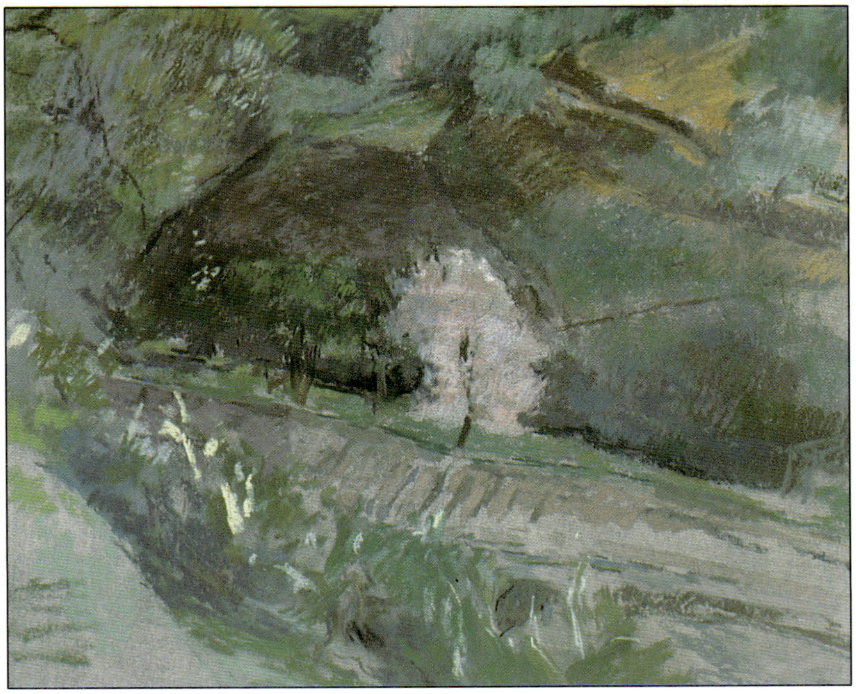

A focus for the eye

(Right) *Not all landscape paintings have an obvious centre of interest, or focal point, but often you will find that you are drawn to a particular view because of some dominant feature. In James Crittenden's* Almond Blossom in the Evening *the focal point is the pale tree, and he has drawn attention to it by using dark neutral colours for the hills beyond. To balance the light tone of the tree, he has introduced strong highlights on the grass on the left of the picture.*

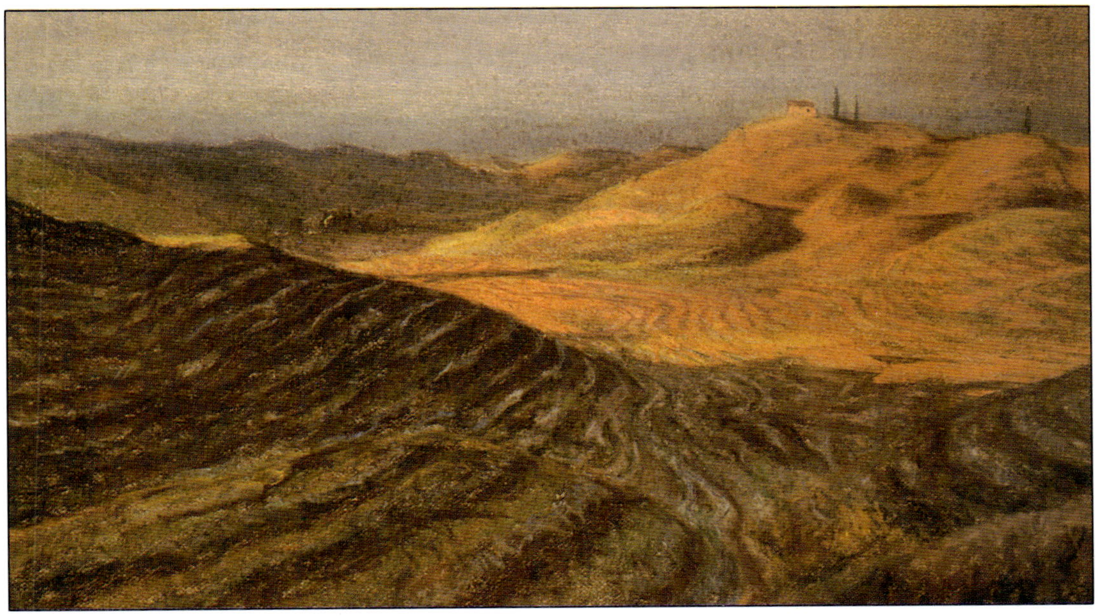

Preliminary sketches

(Left) *Some landscape painters always work out of doors directly from their subject, taking the composition as they find it, while others prefer to compose their paintings in the studio from sketches, notes and sometimes photographs. Patrick Cullen's* Landscape in Le Crete *is a sketch for a very large-scale watercolour painting, which would have been impossible to complete on the spot. The directness of pastel makes it an ideal sketching medium.*

Working indoors

As it can be so difficult to compose paintings in front of the subject, a traditional way of working is to make a sketch or a series of sketches on the spot and compose the actual painting indoors. Often something you haven't quite pulled off can become the basis for a successful composition, so never throw away sketches, even if you are not happy with them. Working indoors removes some of the pressure, giving you the opportunity to think about how best to plan the painting, mix the colours and use the range of pastel marks in the context of the picture. Like brushstrokes in an oil painting, pastel marks are an important ingredient in composition; they are not just an "extra". Vigour and movement in a landscape painting can be conveyed by varying your strokes to include, perhaps, some sweeping directional side strokes, juxtaposed with more linear marks, short jabs and calligraphic squiggles (made with the tip of the pastel).

DEMONSTRATION

Artist Patrick Cullen specializes in landscapes, particularly the scenery of Tuscany, the subject of this painting. He works in oil and watercolour as well as pastel, usually on a large scale, composing his paintings in the studio from sketch references made on the spot. This pastel painting on sandpaper was done from colour sketches and a large charcoal "working drawing" in which he planned the composition.

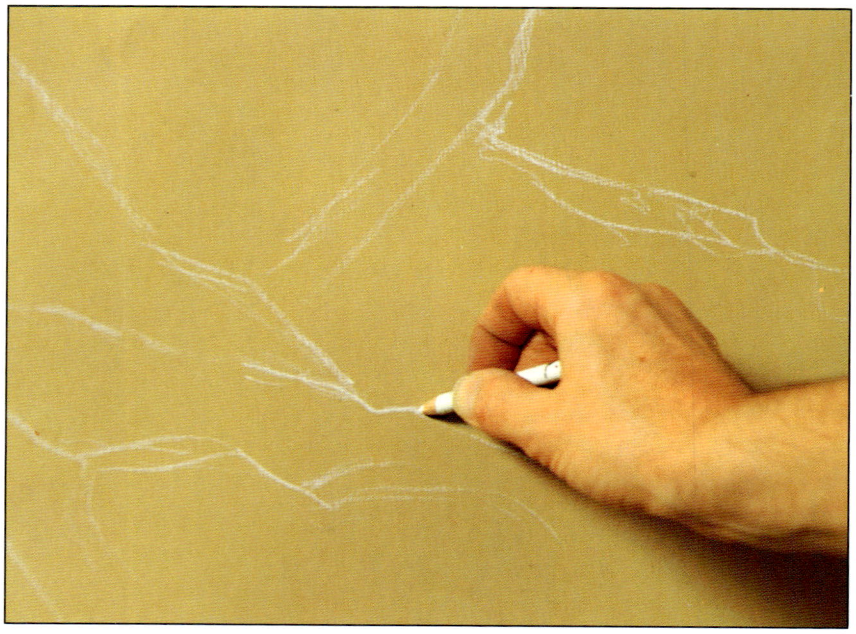

1 *Referring to his charcoal drawing, which is the same size as the painting, the artist begins by mapping out the composition in pastel pencil. He works carefully, as it is impossible to erase pastel marks on sandpaper.*

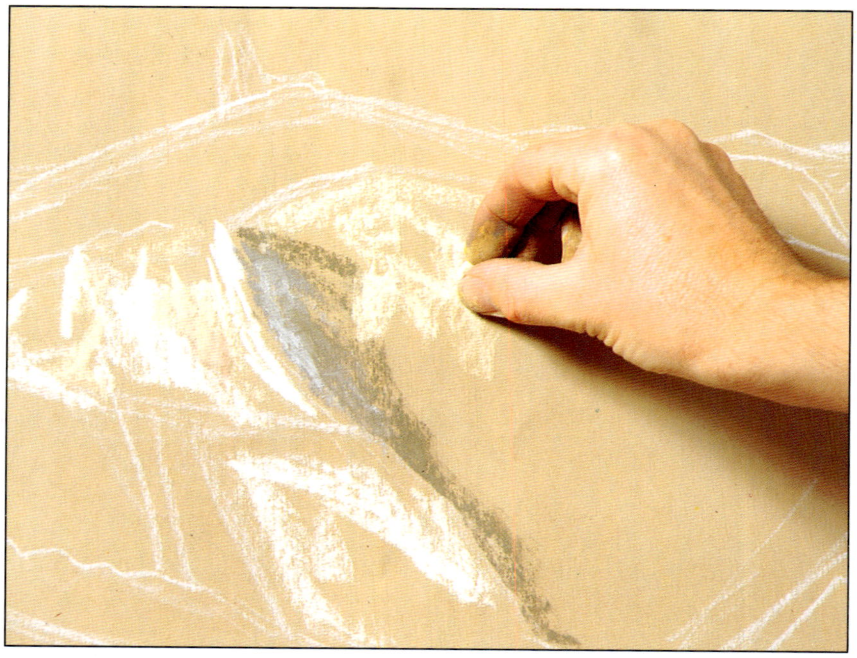

2 *Sandpaper is unlike the standard pastel papers in that colours cannot be moved around to any great extent on the surface. Consequently, the artist works on each section of the picture separately, beginning with the mountains in the centre.*

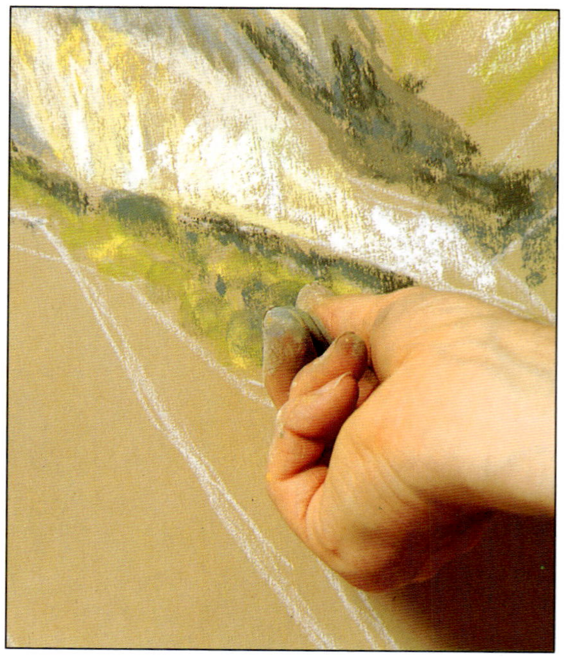

3 *To create the textured effect of the foliage, he pushes his thumb into the pastel colour and twists it. He uses his fingers a good deal in the course of a painting.*

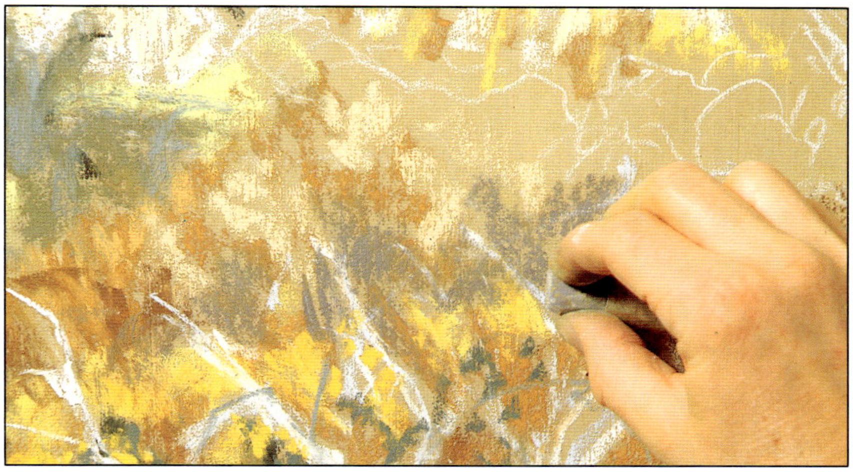

4 *The marks made by the pastel sticks are as important as brushwork in an oil painting; here you can see a wide variety of different strokes, from short jabs to tapering side strokes and crisp linear marks. These impart a lively energy to the picture as well as suggesting shapes and textures.*

5 *This illustration clearly shows the artist's method of working from the centre outwards. This piece-by-piece approach is unusual and is not recommended for beginners, as it involves having a clear vision of how the finished picture will look.*

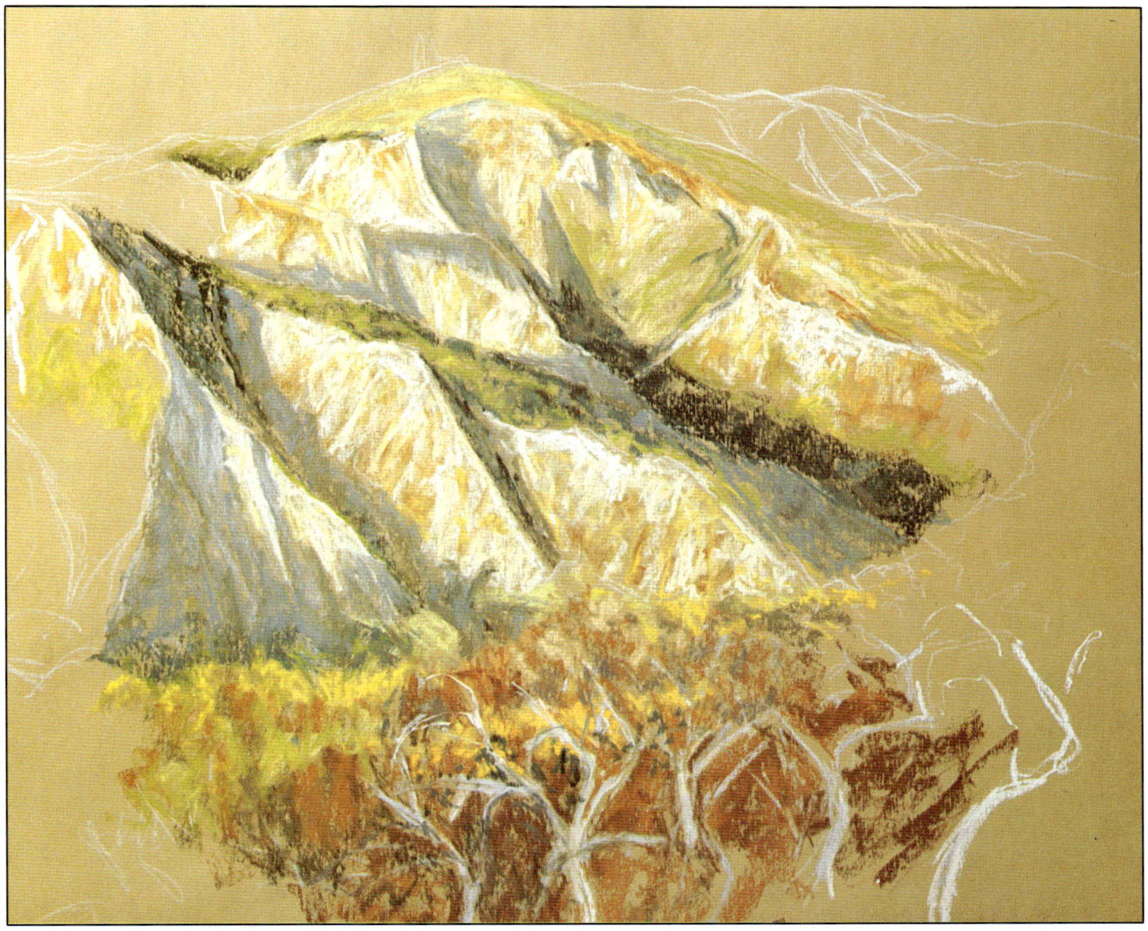

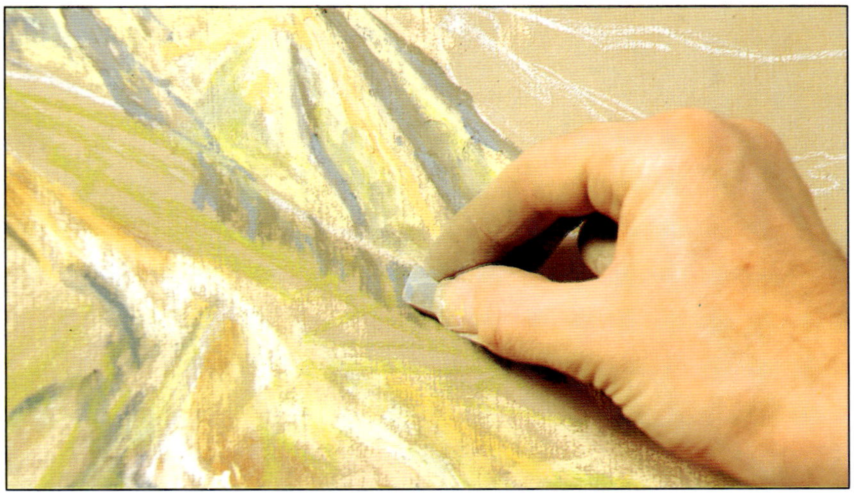

6 *The edge of a broken pastel stick is used to make short, jabbing marks, contrasting with the long sweeping strokes elsewhere. Notice how the paper shows through between strokes, contributing to the overall colour effect.*

Continued ▷

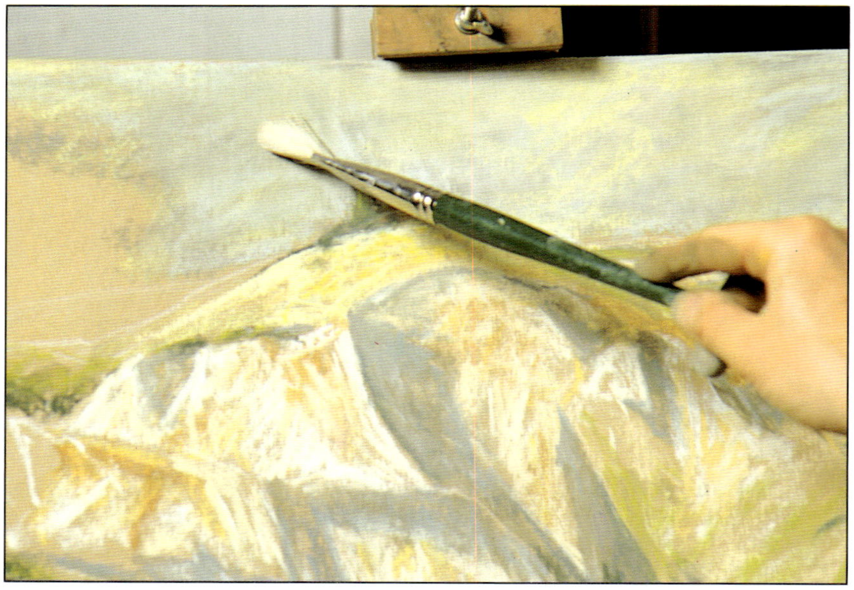

7 Leaving the sky until a late stage enables the artist to assess it in the context of the whole painting. He chooses yellows and pale blue-greys which echo the colours of the mountains. A bristle brush is used to blend the colours together slightly.

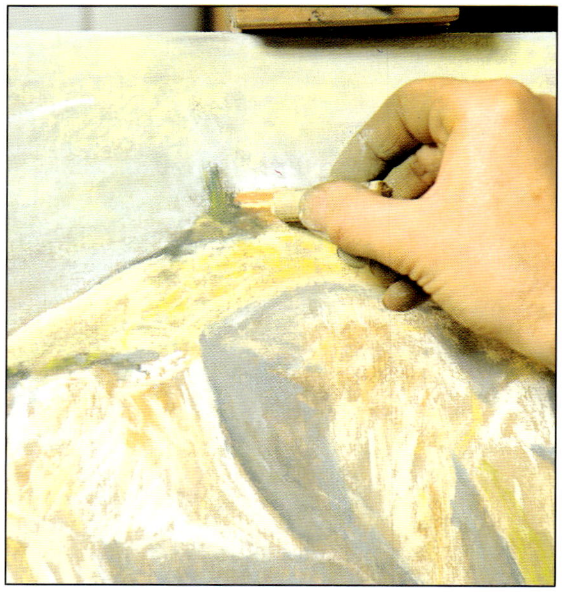

8 Further pale colours have now been dragged lightly over the original ones in the sky area, and the house is drawn with the tip of a pastel stick. Although small, the building is important to the composition because it provides a focus for the eye; you can see this in the finished painting.

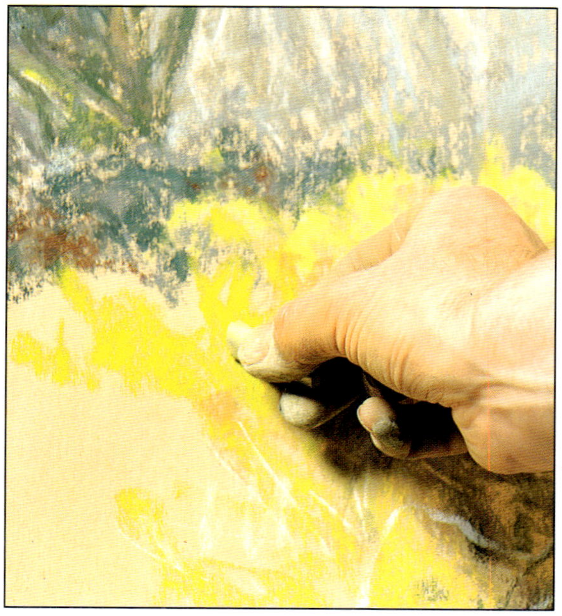

9 On the right-hand side of the painting, the area above the white trees is developed with short strokes of green and yellow, following different directions to create a sense of movement.

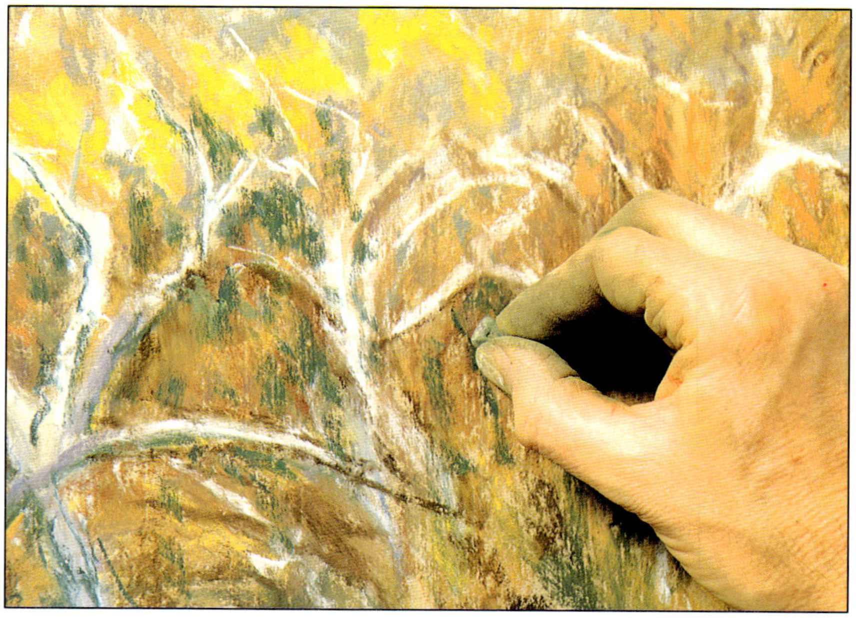

10 The painting is now nearing completion, but requires some crisp touches and bright colours in the foreground to bring it forward in space. Vivid green is used both to suggest leaves and to outline some of the branches.

11 (Right) *Again the artist exploits the contrast between hard and soft edges, now using the side of a short length of pastel to drag colour lightly above and around the branches.*

12 (Below) *Although the painting was virtually completed in one working session, the artist re-assessed it a day or two later and made some adjustments. The most significant of these was to increase the height of the trees on the right so that the white branches lead the eye in towards the dark tree-clad crevice, thus creating a visual link between foreground and distance.*

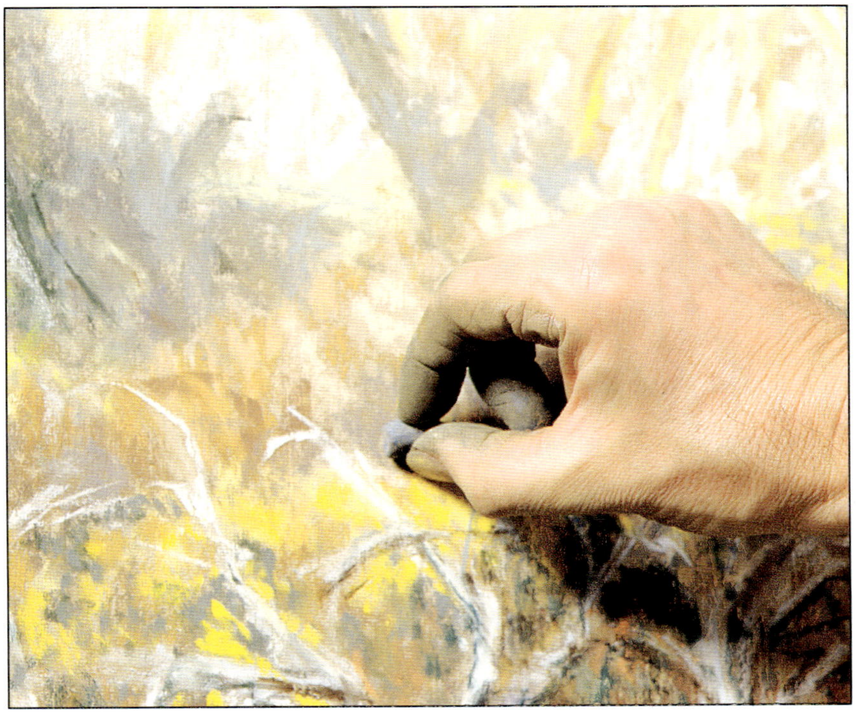

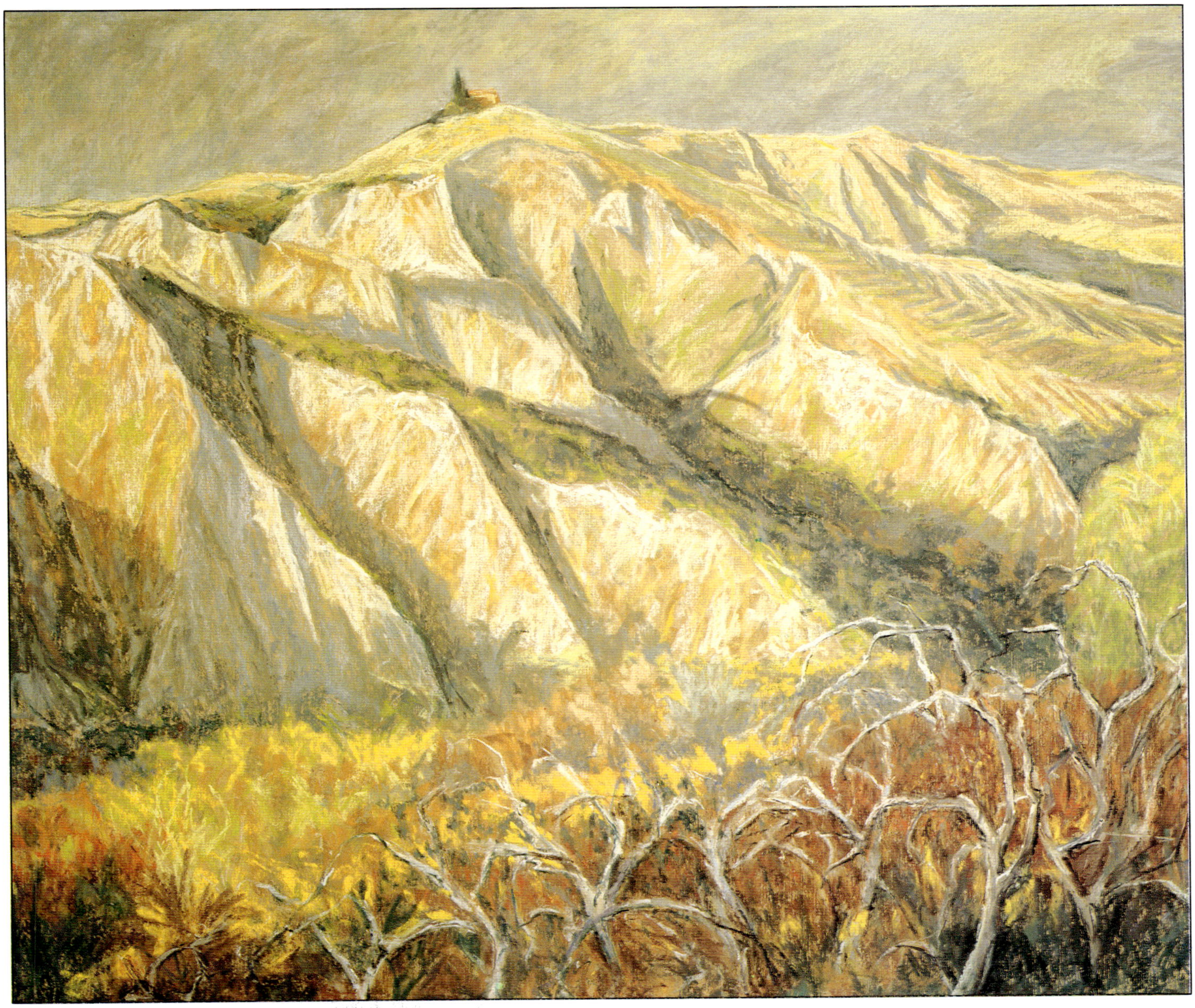

Focus

FLOWERS

When you open a new box of pastels you see an array of brilliant colours which suggests flowers, even before you have begun to put them on the paper. The soft, velvety textures also seem to emulate many of those seen in nature.

DRAWING

Flowers are certainly a wonderful subject and there are few pastel painters who have not at some time tried their hand at them. But, of course, there are problems – there always are. One of the most serious is that flowers are quite complex in shape and structure, both individually and *en masse* in an indoor arrangement and, therefore, you need to concentrate on the drawing. In a vase of flowers, for example, where there are many different shapes and colours as well as the vase itself, it is easy to go wrong and produce a painting in which the flowers and stems don't seem to relate to the container, or the flowerheads to the stems. In a watercolour or oil painting you can make a drawing in pencil first, erasing until you are sure you have it right, but you can't do this in pastel as the colour won't cover pencil marks.

You can, however, draw lightly in charcoal or in pastel pencil; the latter may be preferable in some cases as the charcoal could pollute the pastel colours. When working on coloured paper, choose a light-coloured pastel pencil for the drawing, or one that tones in with the overall colour scheme, and keep the drawing as simple as possible. If you are painting flowers in a vase, don't try to draw each individual bloom and stem; look for the overall shape made by the group.

Once you start to lay on the pastel colour, keep it light initially, as you will certainly find you have to change and redefine some of the shapes. Try to build up the painting in large blocks of colour, leaving the details until last. It is difficult to achieve a high degree of detail with soft pastels, and pastel pencils or hard pastels may be helpful, when you come to the final stages. Meticulous attention to detail sometimes proves unnecessary anyway; pastel is essentially a medium for broad effects and it is often enough just to crispen the edge of a leaf or stem, here and there.

PATTERN

Flowers have an innate pattern element, hence their extensive use as motifs in all the applied arts, from embroidery and printed fabric to ceramics and china. Flowers in a

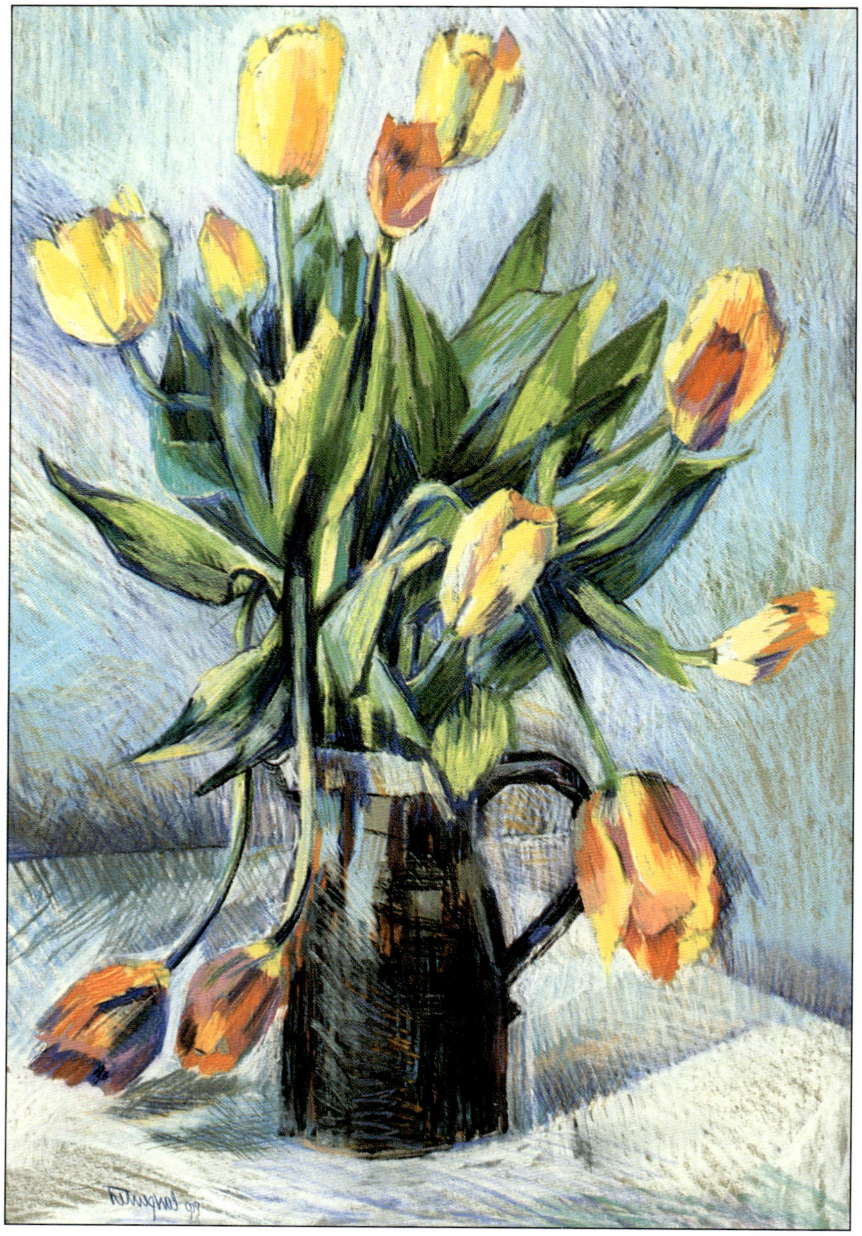

Unity through technique
(Above) *Pip Carpenter has carried the shapes of the flowers and leaves through into the background by using the same kind of strokes for both. This sets up a lively pattern all over the picture surface which enhances the feeling of movement. Jackie Simmonds has used a different technique in her still life* (opposite, above), *linking various elements by repeating colours.*

Unity through colour

(Below) *Although a large mixed bunch of flowers makes an attractive display, it is not always easy to tackle in a painting, as too many colours tend to fight with each other. It is often advisable to set up a group which has one dominant colour, as Jackie Simmonds has done in* Blue Marbles. *To maintain the coherence of the composition, she has repeated the deep blue of the marbles in various places on both of the pots, and has introduced blue into the background.*

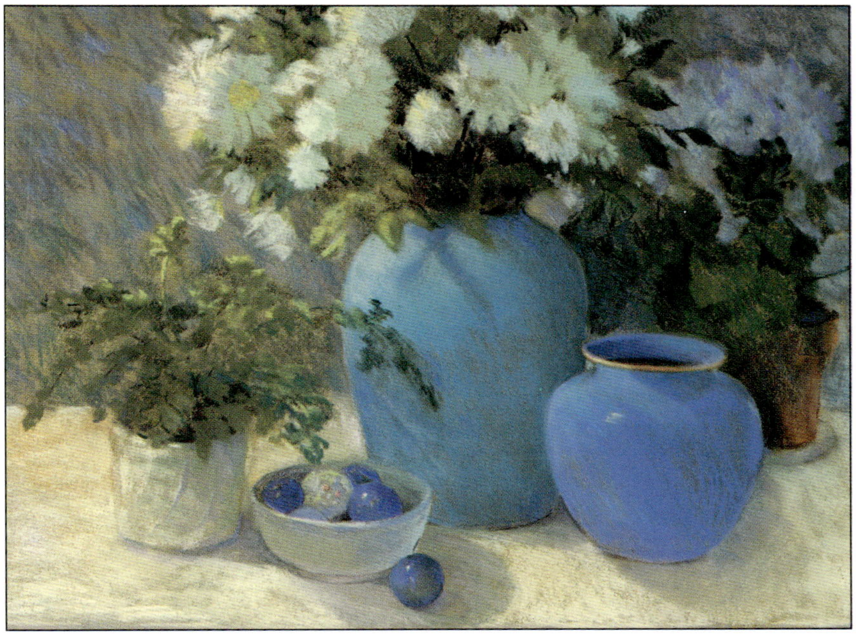

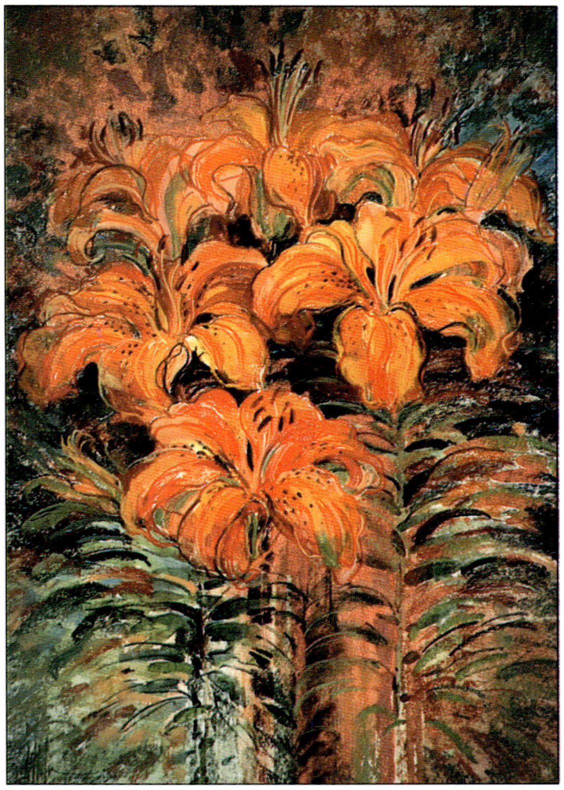

Avoiding overworking

(Above) *The essence of flowers is freshness, and overworked or clogged colour can quickly destroy the impression. In* Orange Lilies, *Maureen Jordan has avoided the necessity of a heavy build-up of pastel by working on an acrylic underpainting. This has allowed her to establish the main colours with thin washes of paint, over which she has worked crisp, linear pastel strokes which beautifully describe the convoluted shapes of the petals.*

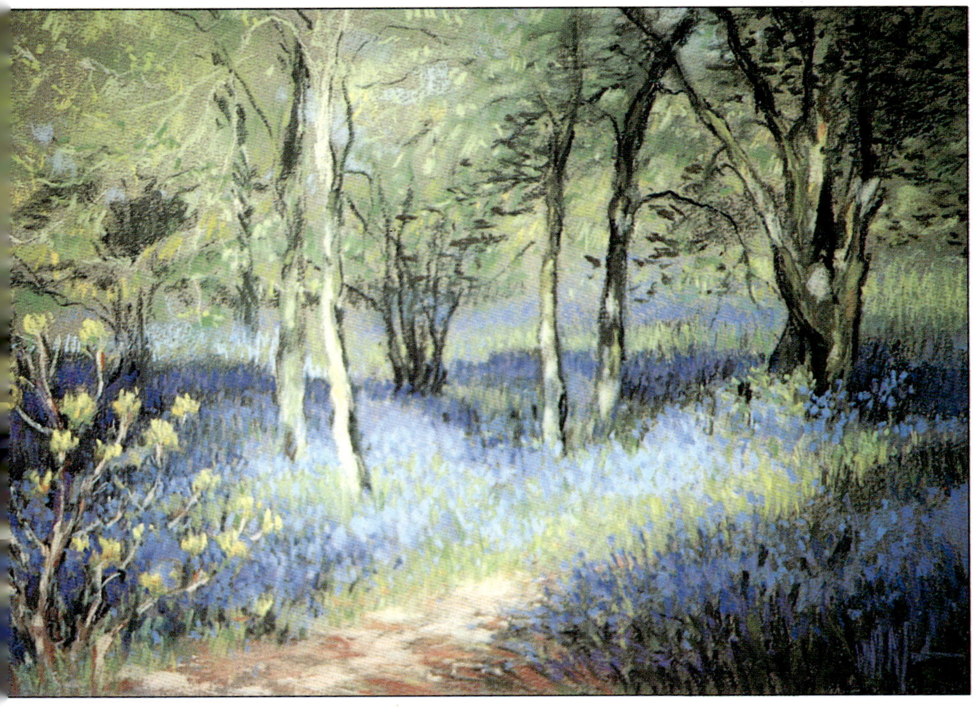

Flowers in landscape

(Left) *When flowers form only one element in a picture they usually need to be treated more broadly and simply than they would in an indoor group. The important features are the overall colour and the growth habit of the flowers. In* Bluebells at Isabella *by Maureen Jordan there is very little detail; even the flowers in the foreground are no more than small dots and dashes of pastel, yet they are immediately recognizable to anyone who has seen a bluebell wood.*

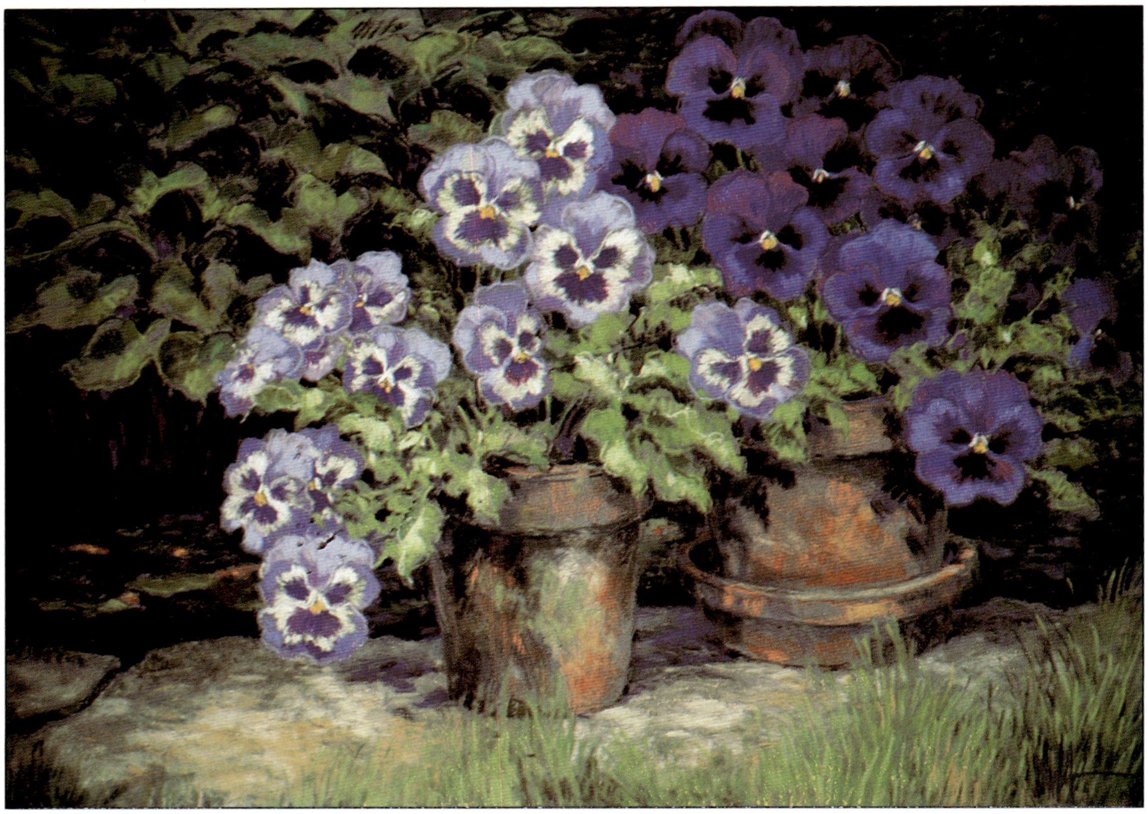

Light on dark
(Left) *A traditional way of painting white or light-coloured flowers is to set them against a dark background, which allows the artist to make the most of their delicacy and subtle nuances of colour. In* Jokers by the Pond, *Maureen Jordan has used the same idea but in an outdoor setting, with the sun and shade providing both excellent definition and contrasts of tone.*

vase create a pattern through the interaction of the various shapes and colours; you can stress this in your painting in a variety of ways. Attention can be drawn to the colour and pattern of an elaborate floral arrangement by setting it against a plain backdrop, perhaps even working on dark-coloured paper and leaving it uncovered in some areas. Alternatively, you can carry the pattern element right through the painting, choosing a decorated container for the flowers, and setting them against a wallpaper or some draped fabric with its own patterns and textures.

The way in which you use the pastel is also important in this context. You can create pattern as well as a sense of movement by letting the pastel strokes show in an active and positive way, rather than blending colours together. You might use strong, directional strokes for leaves and stems and, in the background, let the pastel stick follow the direction of the flowers to create a network of curving or vertical lines in different colours. As flowers are soft and delicate, there is always a tendency to over-blend, but bear in mind that this is not always the best approach.

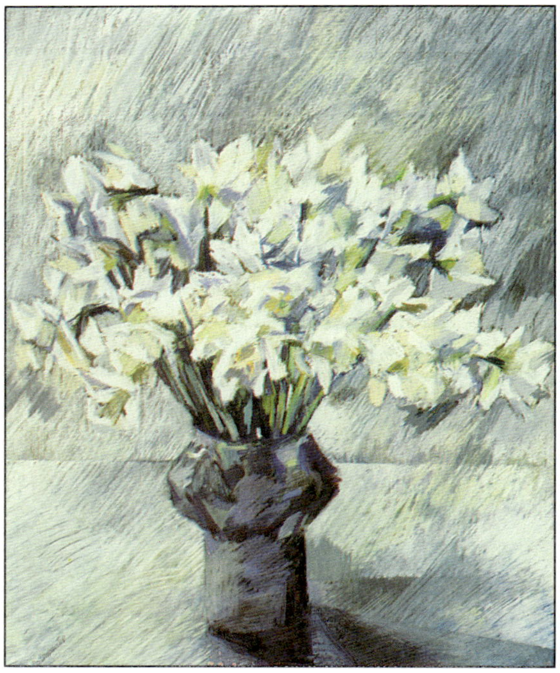

Light on light
(Above) *An alternative approach for white or pale flowers is to set them against a white background and exploit the tonal contrasts in the flowers themselves, as Pip Carpenter has done in* White Daffodils. *Although the vase and the stems are the only genuinely dark areas, she has cleverly made use of shadows on the petals and subtle contrasts in the background, and has also played up the foreground shadow to balance the dark vase. It is surprising how many dark and middle tones can be seen in white.*

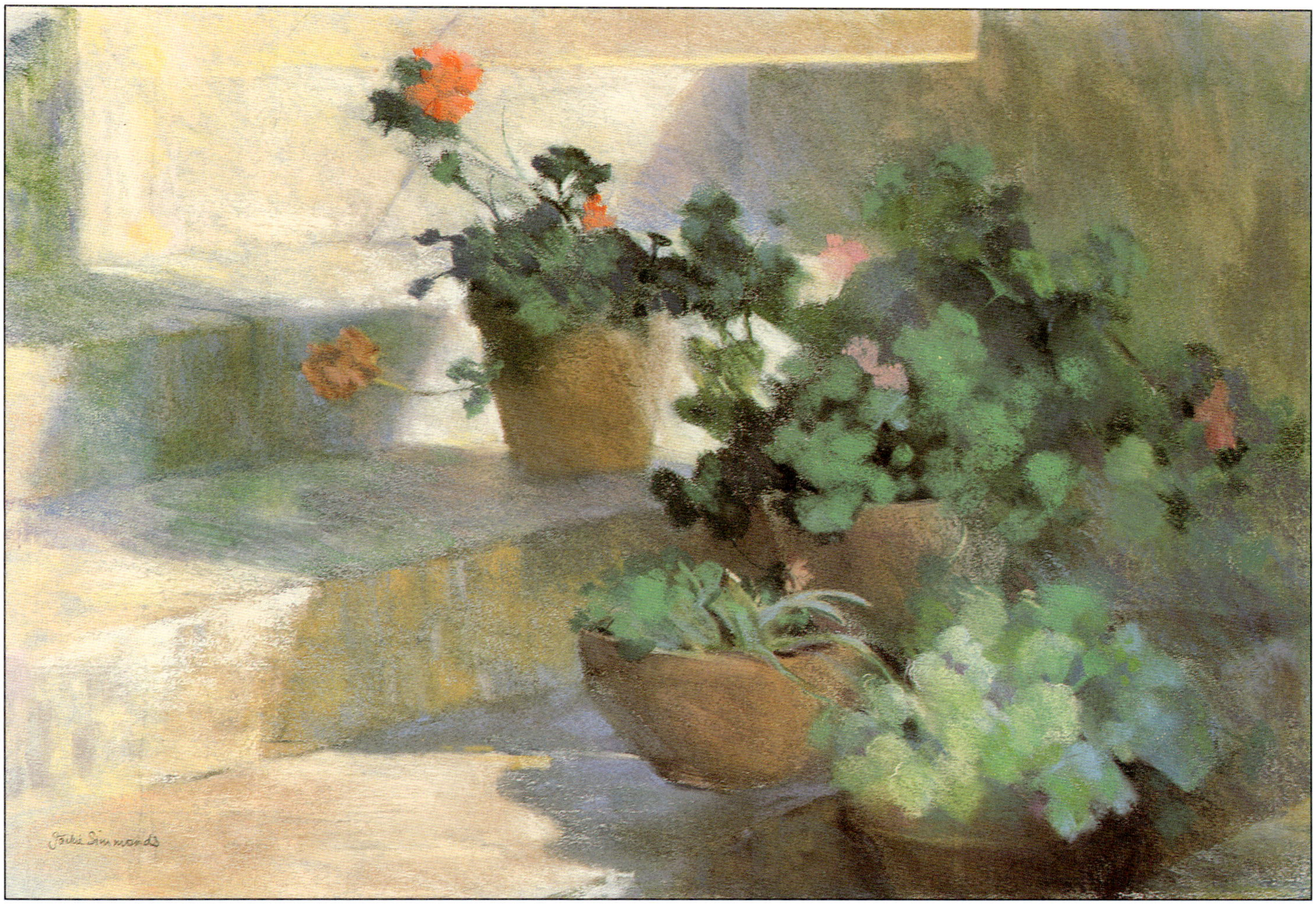

Complementary colours
(Above) *The colours opposite one another on a colour wheel – red and green, yellow and violet, orange and blue – are called complementaries, and they play an important part in painting as they set up exciting contrasts when used together. In Jackie Simmonds's* Tuscany Steps, *the red and green complementary pair was built into the subject, but she has also used yellow/violet contrasts for both the plant pots and the steps to create areas of vibrant colour.*

HABITAT

Although the phrase "flower painting" tends to conjure up images of indoor arrangements, flowers in their natural setting can also make a rewarding subject. Whether it be garden flowers or wild flowers in a field, woodland or a patch of urban wasteland, the choice is yours. You cannot, of course, control the set-up or plan the colour scheme in advance, but you have a wide range of options with regard to composition and general approach.

Flowers in a garden or field, for example, could be treated as broad masses of colour or as colour accents in a landscape; alternatively, if you are interested in the shapes and colours of individual flowers, you could focus in more closely, making one or two blooms the subject of your painting. If you decide to make outdoor "portraits" of flowers, you must be aware of possible changes in the light but, as pastel allows you to build up colour effects very quickly, the problem is less acute than it might be in watercolour or oil painting.

Finally, don't ignore the fact that trees have flowers too; few subjects have more appeal than an orchard or a single blossom tree in spring. Here too you could take a close-up view and paint a single bough of blossom – the Oriental painters loved such effects. Trees with large and well-shaped flowers, such as magnolia, are particularly well-suited to this kind of treatment.

DEMONSTRATION

Rosalind Cuthbert works in a number of different media and subject areas – flowers are one of her interests, but she also paints portraits and landscapes. Her light and delicate pastel style is well suited to this elegant and colourful arrangement of tall flowers. She is working on smooth-surfaced watercolour paper, which she prefers to the medium-textured paper because it does not break up the strokes to the same extent, thus allowing for clear, crisp lines.

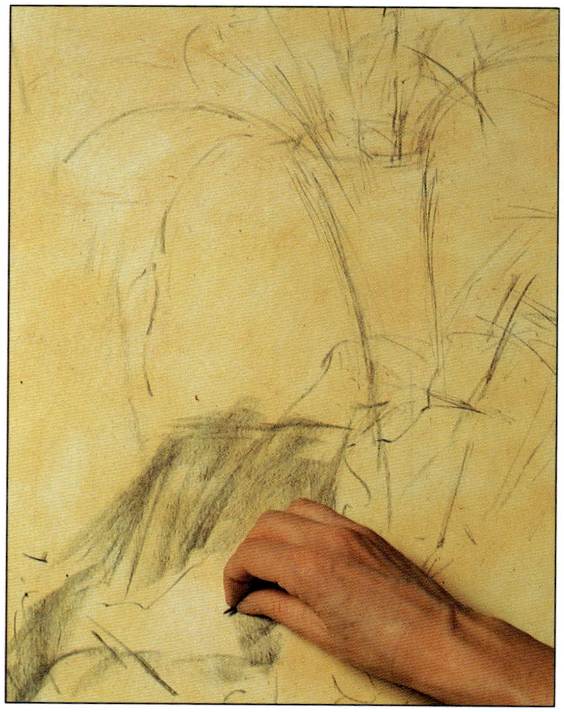

1 *The paper has been tinted using the dry-wash method. Yellow is the dominant colour in the painting, so the artist has chosen a deep yellow for the ground. She now draws the main shapes lightly in charcoal.*

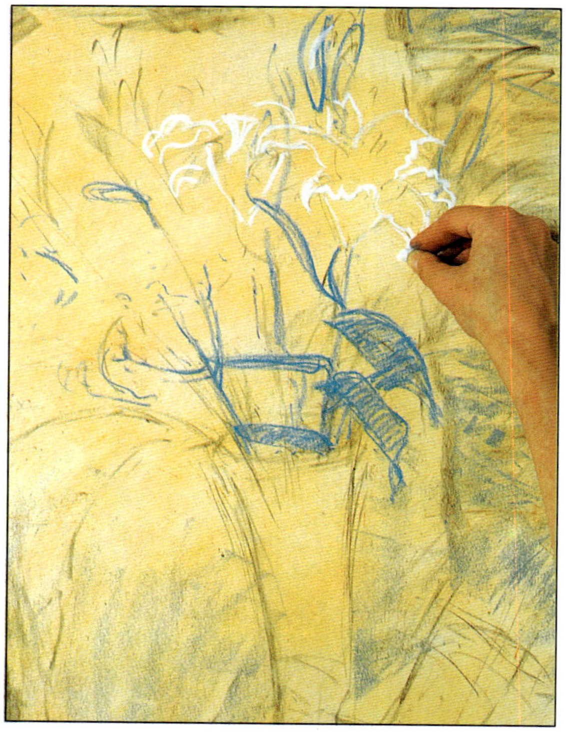

2 *Having sketched in the leaves lightly with linear strokes of blue, she now draws the outlines of the two pink-and-white lilies with the tip of the pastel stick. Her method is to build up colours with a series of light overlays; the blue leaves will be modified later using other colours.*

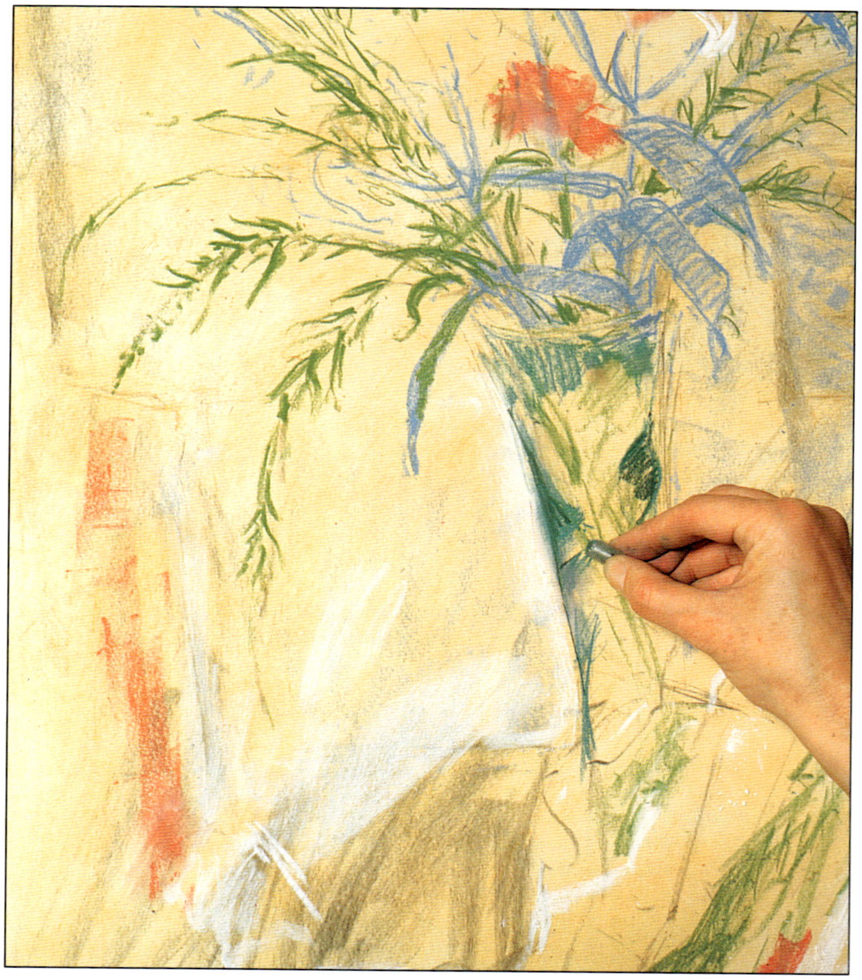

3 (Right) *It is important not only to define the shape of the vase at an early stage but also to establish a balance of light and dark colours. In this area she works with the tip of the pastel, although some light side strokes can be seen in the background, where softer effects are needed.*

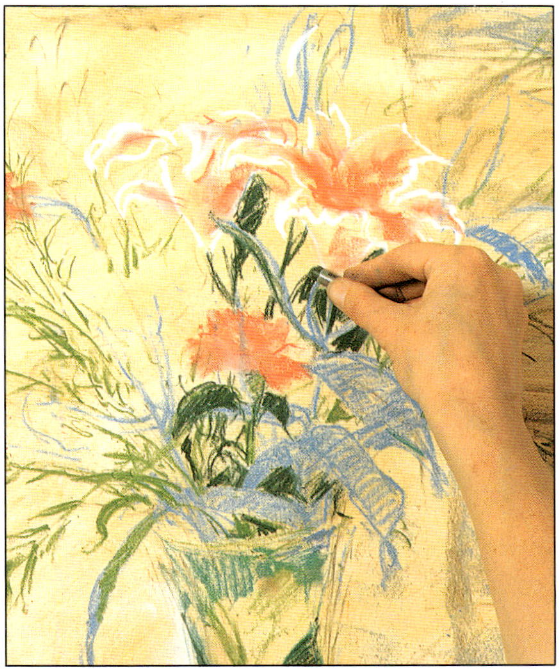

4 *These dark leaves play an important part in the picture, as the light–dark contrast between them and the flowerheads draws the eye to this central area.*

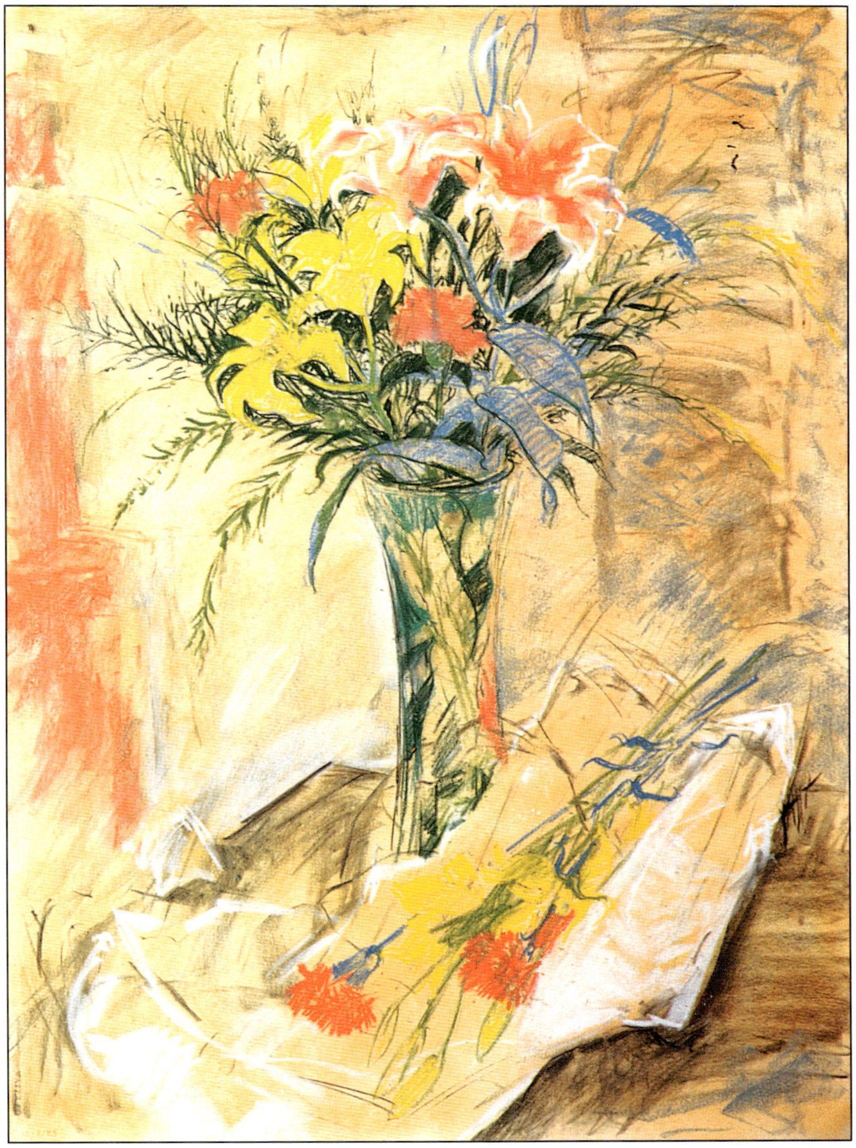

5 (Right) *The painting has now reached approximately halfway stage, with all the colours blocked in. The artist has been careful to work lightly and loosely to allow for later applications of colour and refinements of detail.*

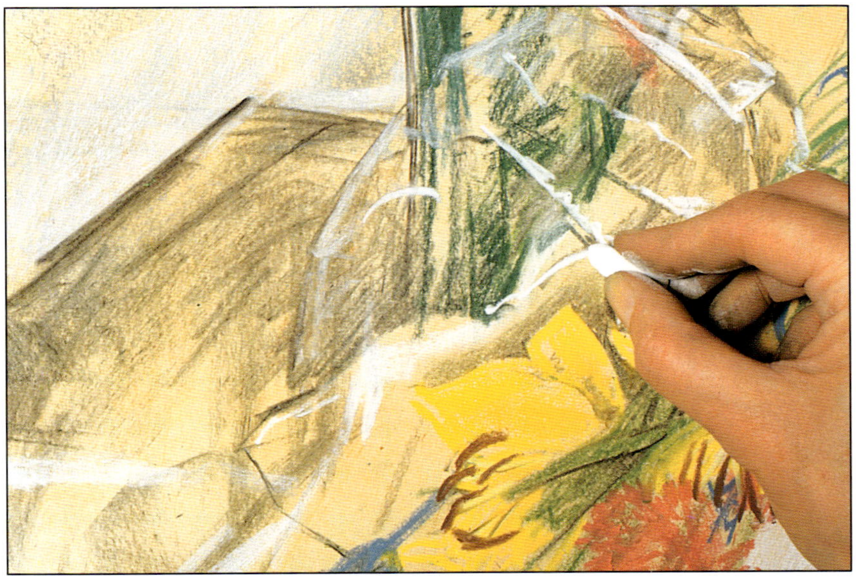

6 *The foreground, which had been left relatively undefined, is now sharpened up with a crisp drawing of the piece of crumpled wrapping.*

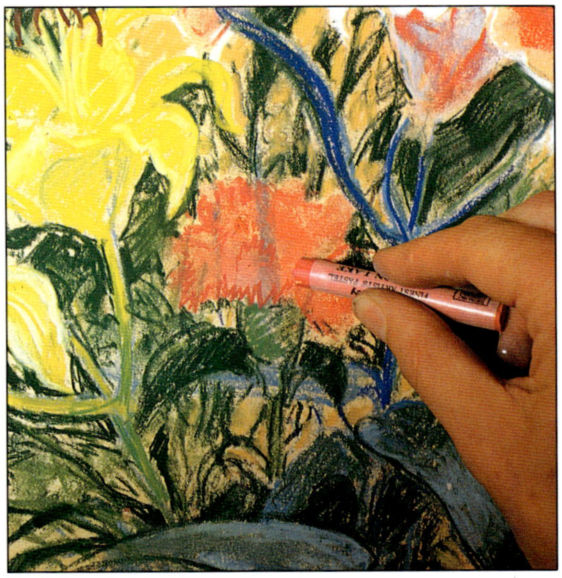

7 *The frilly-edged petals of these carnations are suggested by linear marks drawn with a darker version of the original pink.*

Continued ▷

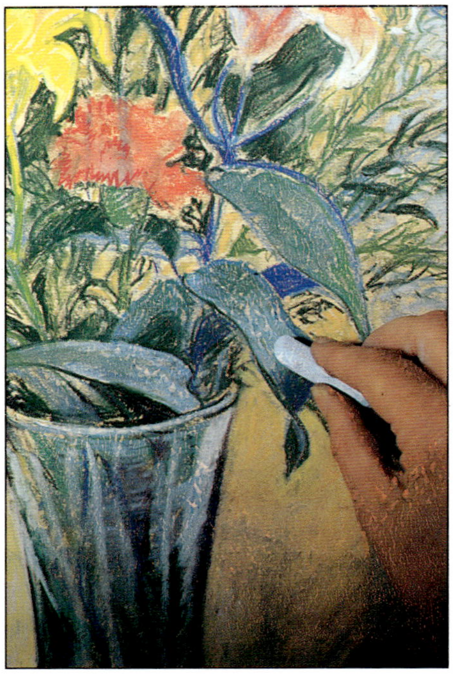

8 *The original blue used for the leaves has been overlaid with other colours and blended slightly to imitate their smooth texture. The pale grey, here used thickly for the highlights, also appears on the vase.*

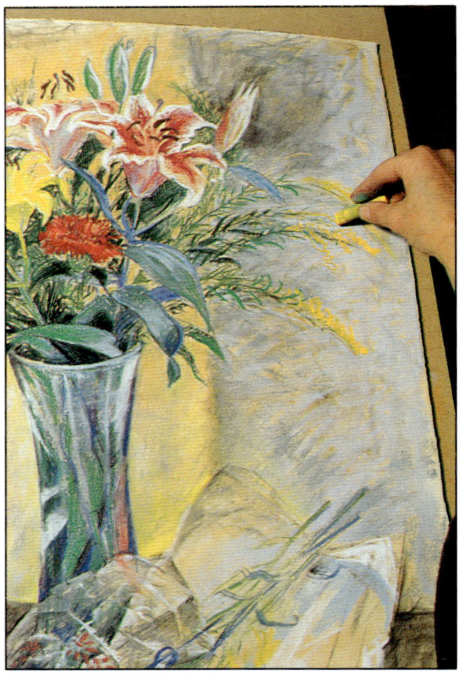

9 *The dominant colour, yellow, is carried right through the painting, appearing in a paler version in both background and foreground. The pale grey background allows these small flowers to stand out, but they are treated lightly because the central flowers are the main focus for the eye.*

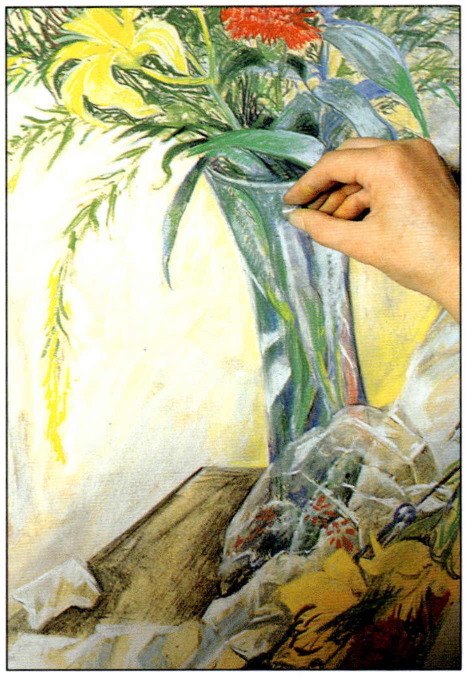

10 *The colours of the vase were too smoothly blended and were losing their liveliness and freshness, so small linear strokes are laid on top. This treatment has also set up a relationship between the vase and the leaves above.*

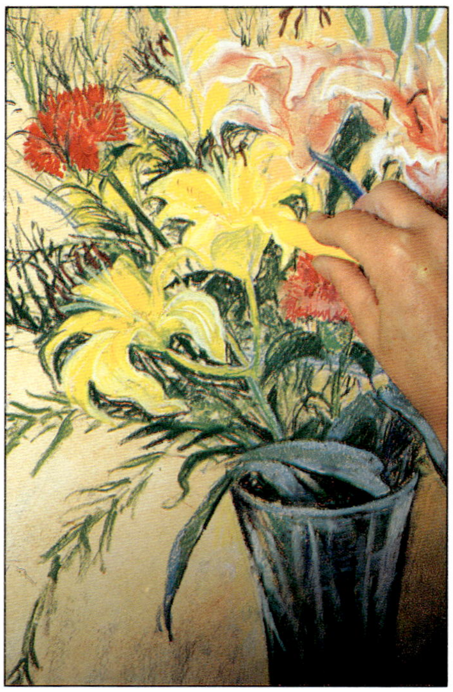

11 *The flowers have been built up with layers of colour and occasional soft outlines, some made with hard pastel. A soft deep yellow pastel is now used to work carefully within the paler yellow edges of the petals.*

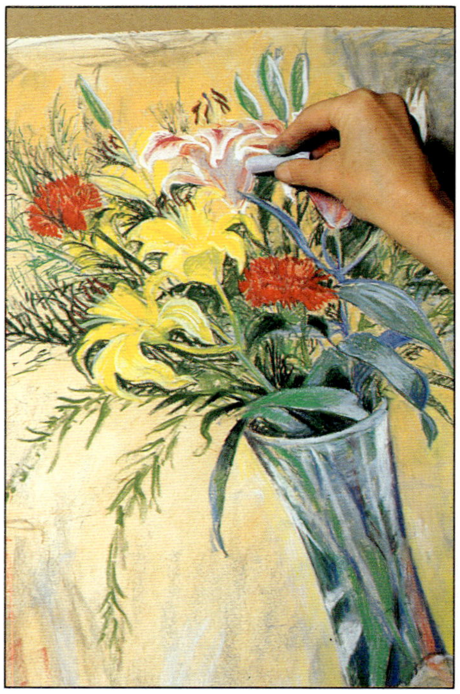

12 *A stick of hard pastel has been used to create a series of little broken lines on the petals of the pink-and-white lily. The underside is now toned down with grey, which mixes with the underlying pink to form a delicate mauve.*

13 (Opposite) *Painting a group of tall flowers can cause problems of composition unless there is something in the foreground to create interest and to balance the shape of the vase. The artist has solved this by using the table top and the shape made by the wrapping paper as positive elements. The background, although lightly treated, is also carefully contrived, with the grey and red shapes at either side both balancing and enclosing the flowers and vase.*

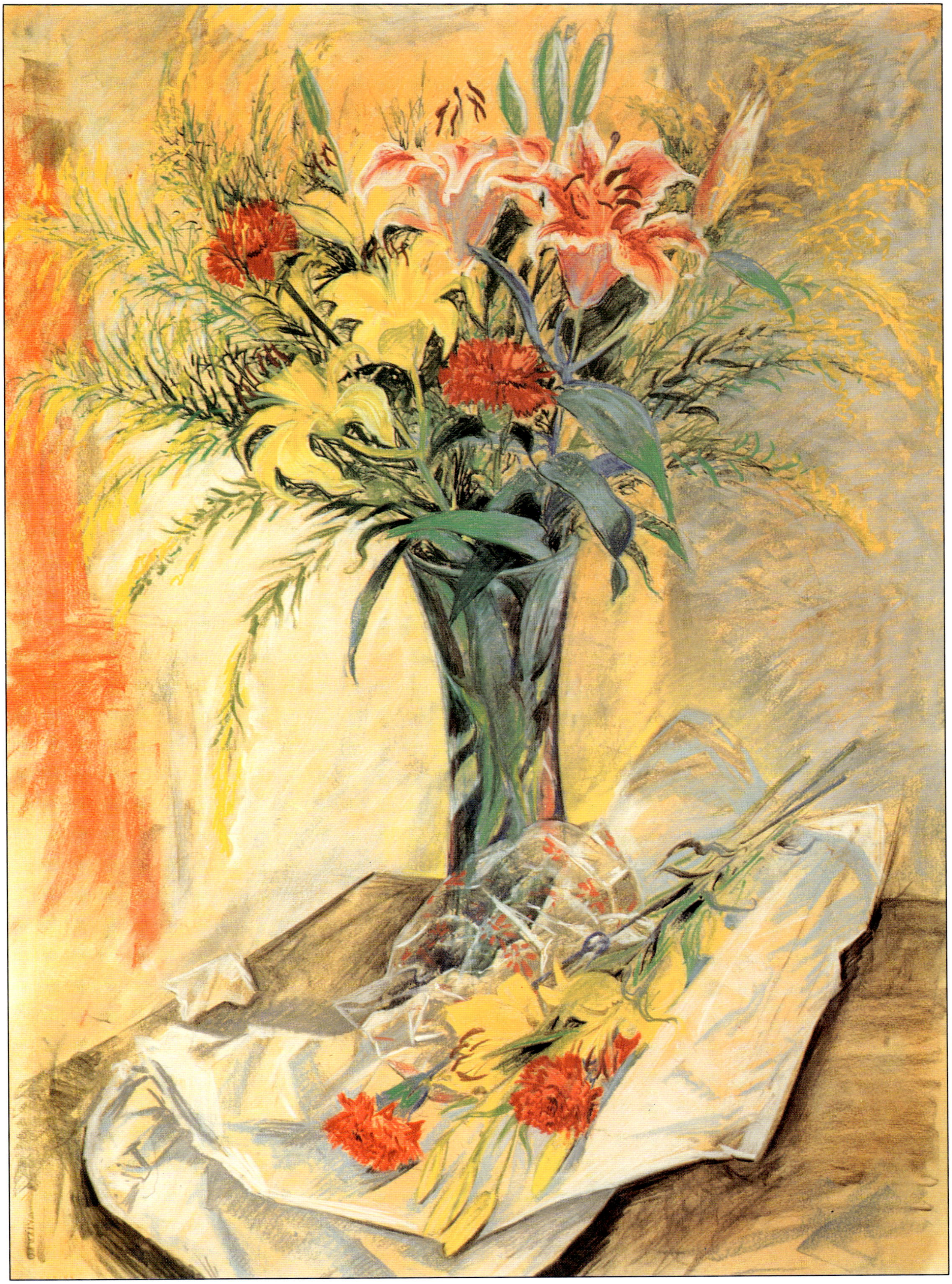

FACES & FIGURES

Pastel seems tailor-made for portraits and figure paintings because of the way in which it doubles as a drawing and a painting medium. The range and versatility of pastel enables you to build up forms with broad areas of colour as well as to exploit different kinds of lines and marks. It is also suited both to full-scale finished compositions and to quick sketches.

PORTRAITS

Pastel has been a favoured medium for portraiture since the 18th century, when artists such as Rosalba Carriera and Maurice Quentin de La Tour became fascinated by its capacity for creating soft and delicate effects. Many of today's artists also find it an excellent medium for faces and figures, though the current emphasis is less on the subtle blending of colour than on the expressive quality of pastel marks.

Embarking on a portrait in pastel does require a degree of skill and confidence, as major changes cannot be made. If you find that you have misunderstood the shape and proportion of your subject's features, there is not, unfortunately, a great deal you can do about it. There are, however, some methods that you may find helpful initially, one of these being to work over a tonal underdrawing in charcoal. You can make as many changes as you like to the charcoal drawing because charcoal is easy to rub off and re-apply. Once you are happy with the drawing, you can spray it with fixative and apply the pastel colour on top.

Working on one of the pastel papers which allows you to make corrections by laying one colour over another may also boost your confidence. You can do this to some extent on any paper, but with Sansfix paper or sandpaper you can make quite major alterations.

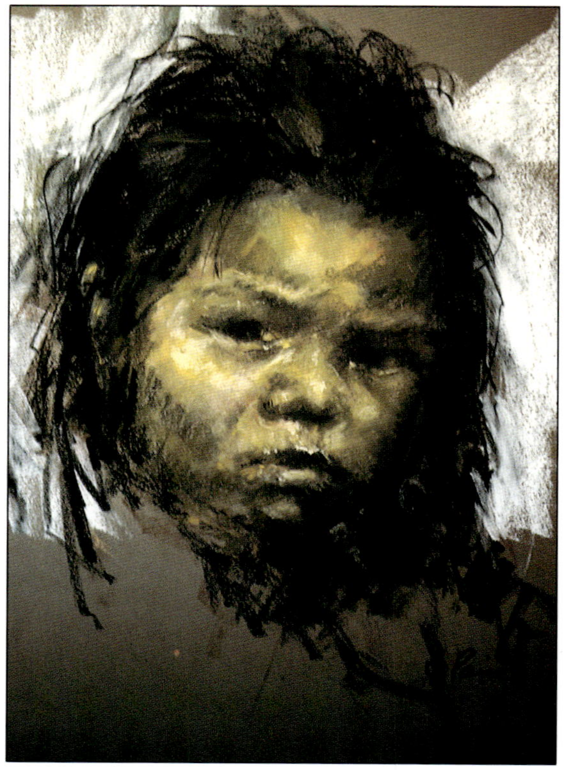

Using the paper colour
(Right) *In portraiture and figure work it is particularly important to choose the right colour of paper, especially if you intend to leave areas of it uncovered, as in Ken Paine's superb* Young Girl. *The painting is almost monochromatic, with the lights and darks built up from the mid-tone of the brown paper.*

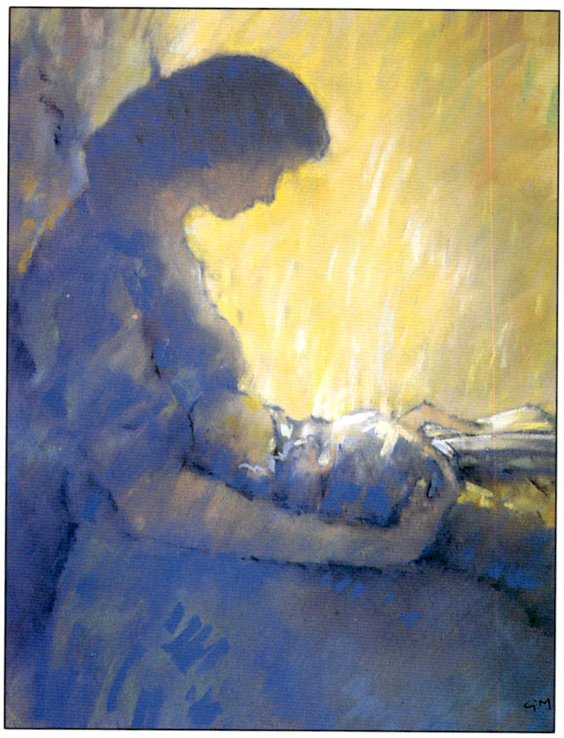

Light and mood
(Left) *For a portrait or figure painting in which it is important to describe features and forms accurately, it is best to choose side or three-quarter lighting, but backlighting can create lovely effects, silhouetting the figure, softening the colours and reducing the tonal contrasts. In his lovely* Mother and Child *Geoff Marsters has exploited this kind of lighting to create a gentle and meditative mood that is entirely in keeping with the subject.*

PRACTISING PORTRAITURE

One of the difficulties with portrait painting is finding someone who is willing to sit for

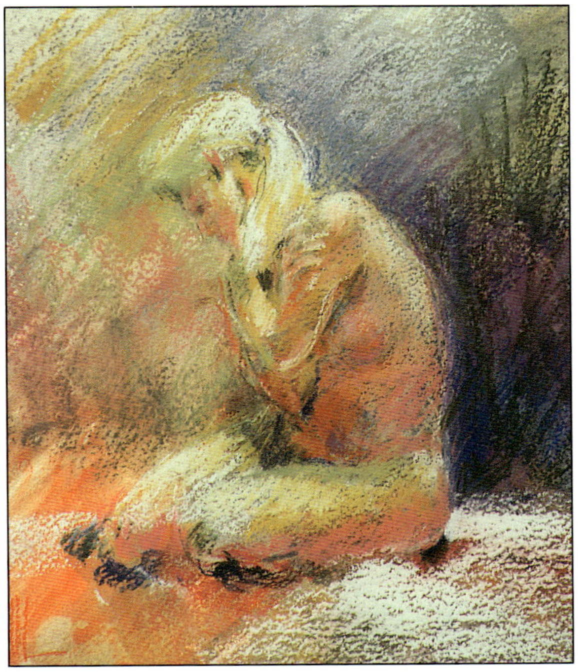

Dramatic light
(Left) *Maureen Jordan has called her painting* In the Spotlight *and, as the title implies, the main subject is light rather than the figure itself, which is treated as a bold, broad generalization. She has applied the pastel thickly, working on textured watercolour paper, which allows a considerable build-up of pigment.*

Painting flesh tones
(Below) *In* Seated Nude *Robert Maxwell Wood has also chosen the paper wisely; it is almost the same colour as the mid-tone of the model's flesh, allowing him to use the pastel lightly and delicately. He has used blending methods in places, but has avoided over-doing this, as it can make the image appear bland and dull. Instead he has contrasted soft blends with crisp diagonal hatching lines and fine outlines made with the tip of the pastel to describe the fall of light on the head, neck and arms.*

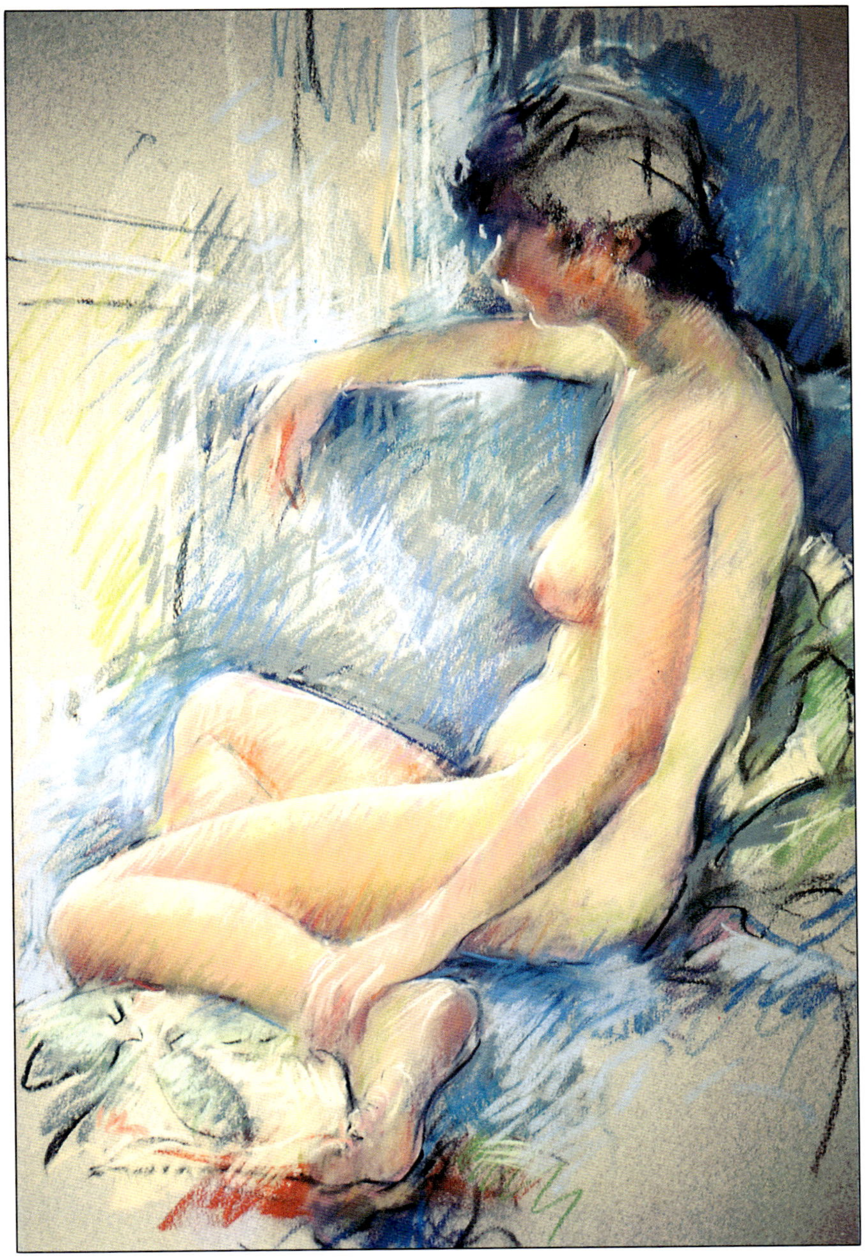

you and who won't be insulted by early and possibly inept attempts! You always have one model on hand, however – yourself. Most artists have painted and drawn self-portraits at times during their careers; this is an excellent way of gaining practice in handling the medium, as well as acquiring confidence in the basic skills of portraiture.

Another good way of learning is to copy another artist's work; up until the end of the 19th century most artists considered this an essential part of their education. It is best to make what are known as "transcriptions", which means choosing a work in another medium, such as oils, as your model. If you try to make a faithful copy of someone else's pastel portrait, it will hinder the development of your own style, added to which, colour mixing will create additional problems because you are unlikely to have the same palette of colours.

You can also learn a lot about composition by copying. Do not only concentrate on trying to reproduce the forms and colours accurately; ask yourself why the artist has arranged the picture in a particular way. You might try making small pencil sketches from several different portraits, which will give you ideas about types of portrait composition. Some portraits, for example, show the whole

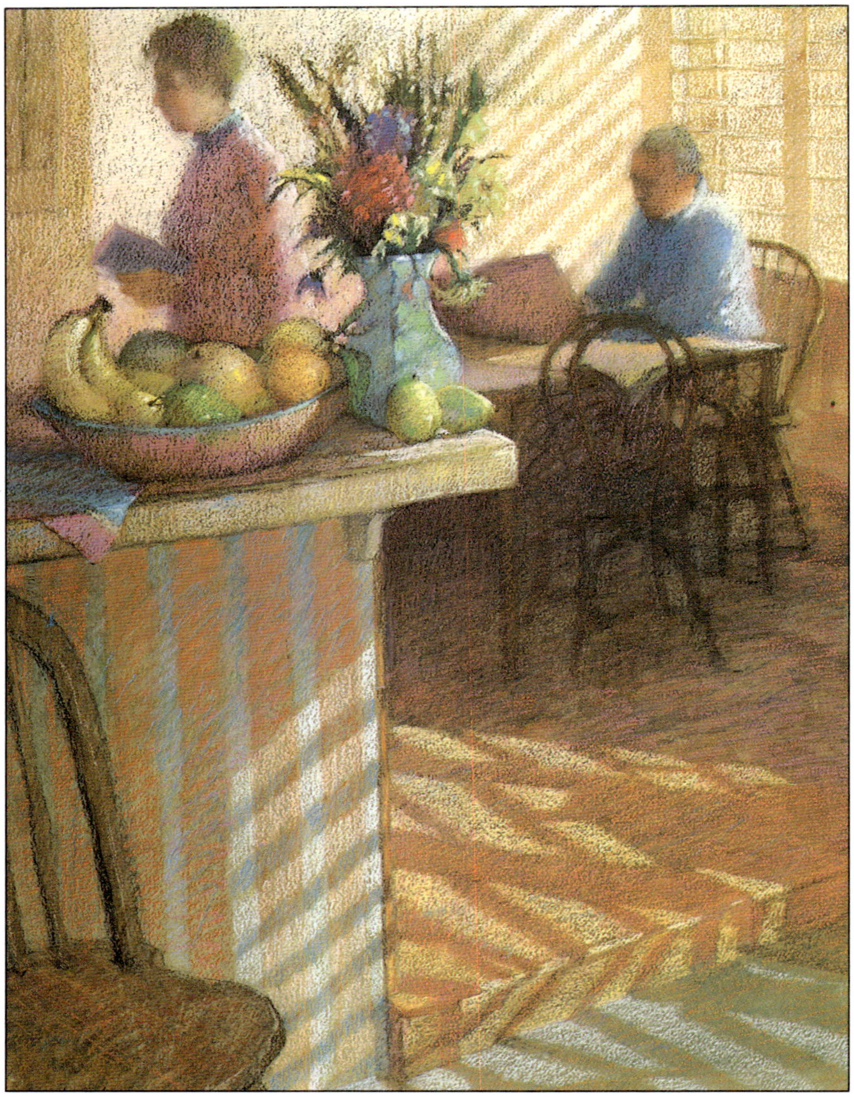

SKETCHING

Although you can sharpen your technical skills and learn to analyse composition by copying, the best practice of all is gained by drawing – as much and as often as possible. If you are drawing people purely for practice, you can use any medium with which you feel comfortable; but sketching has another purpose too: a series of colour sketches made in pastel can give you a good basis for a finished portrait or figure study. Many portraits are carried out from sketches, sometimes with the aid of a photograph to provide more detailed visual information.

Interiors with figures
(Above) *If you are painting a portrait, the face or figure will be the main centre of attention, with other elements such as furniture playing a subsidiary role, but in Sally Strand's* Passing Quietly *the figures are fully integrated into the interior of the room. The real subject of the painting is light and colour, and the people have been treated almost as inanimate objects, echoing the still life on the counter and the chair in the corner.*

figure, standing or seated; other show half or three-quarters of the body including the hands, while many "crop" just below the neck to show only the head and shoulders.

FIGURES IN A SETTING

Figure painting and portrait painting are closely linked, but there is one essential difference. The dictionary definition of a portrait is a "likeness of an individual", while a figure painting, whether it be a nude study or a group of figures in an indoor or outdoor setting, need not necessarily perform this function. This is not to say that the figures should be unrecognizable as individuals. Just as you would want a tree in a landscape to look different from its neighbour, some characteristic of a person should be stressed, but this need not be features – it can be posture, general shape or even the colour of clothing. You might include a figure in a landscape, for example, simply because you want a bright accent of colour, or you might like the stark contrast of tone provided by a dark-clad figure in front of a sunlit whitewashed wall, in a Mediterranean town or village.

There are many reasons for drawing and painting figures other than portraiture, and the human element can be used, not as the whole subject of the painting, but as part of its visual "furniture". This is where the value of sketching really becomes apparent. People never remain in one place for long and you can seldom paint on the spot a landscape or townscape containing figures; such paintings are usually composed from sketches. Photographs are also a useful aid – don't become too reliant on them, but don't under-estimate their value either. Walter Sickert painted many urban scenes and figure compositions from photographs.

Composing the picture

(Right) *Even when you paint a head-and-shoulders portrait you need to consider how to place it on the paper and, in a full-length study, good composition is vitally important. In Maureen Jordan's* Amanda *the figure and sofa arm form a rough triangle, with the slope of the upper body balanced by the opposing line of the thigh. She has given only a hint of definition to the feet, allowing them to "bleed" out of the frame at the bottom so that the viewer's attention is focused on the face and body.*

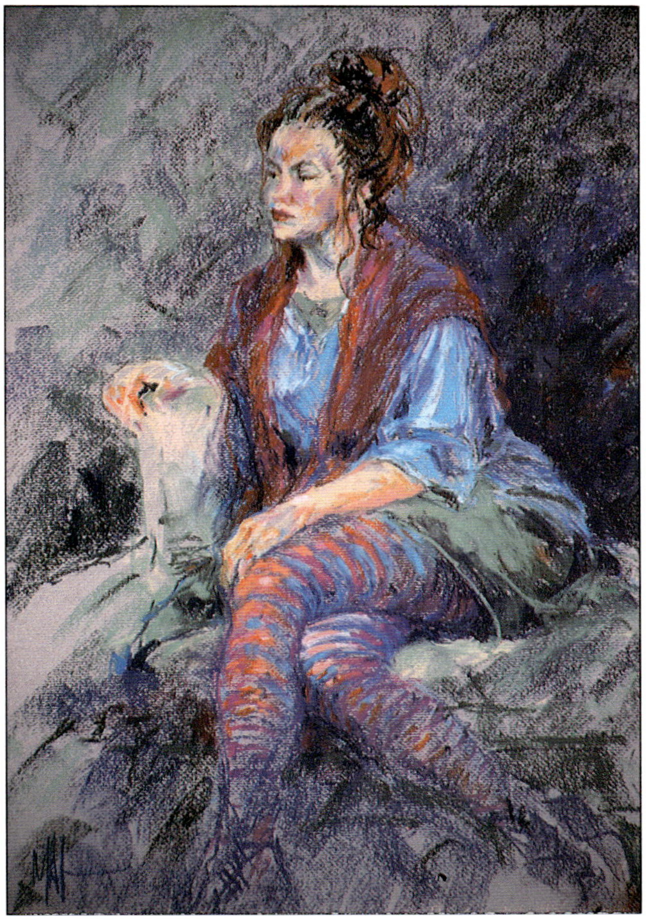

Figure groups

(Below) *In landscape painting, a distant figure or group of figures is often introduced as a colour accent or an additional focus for the eye, but where figures form the whole subject, as in Sally Strand's charming* Crab Catch, *it is necessary to find ways of relating them to one another. Like many such compositions, this has an element of story-telling, with the boys sharing a common interest, but the artist has also used clever pictorial devices, notably the shapes and colours of the towel and bucket, to create a strong link between the two figures.*

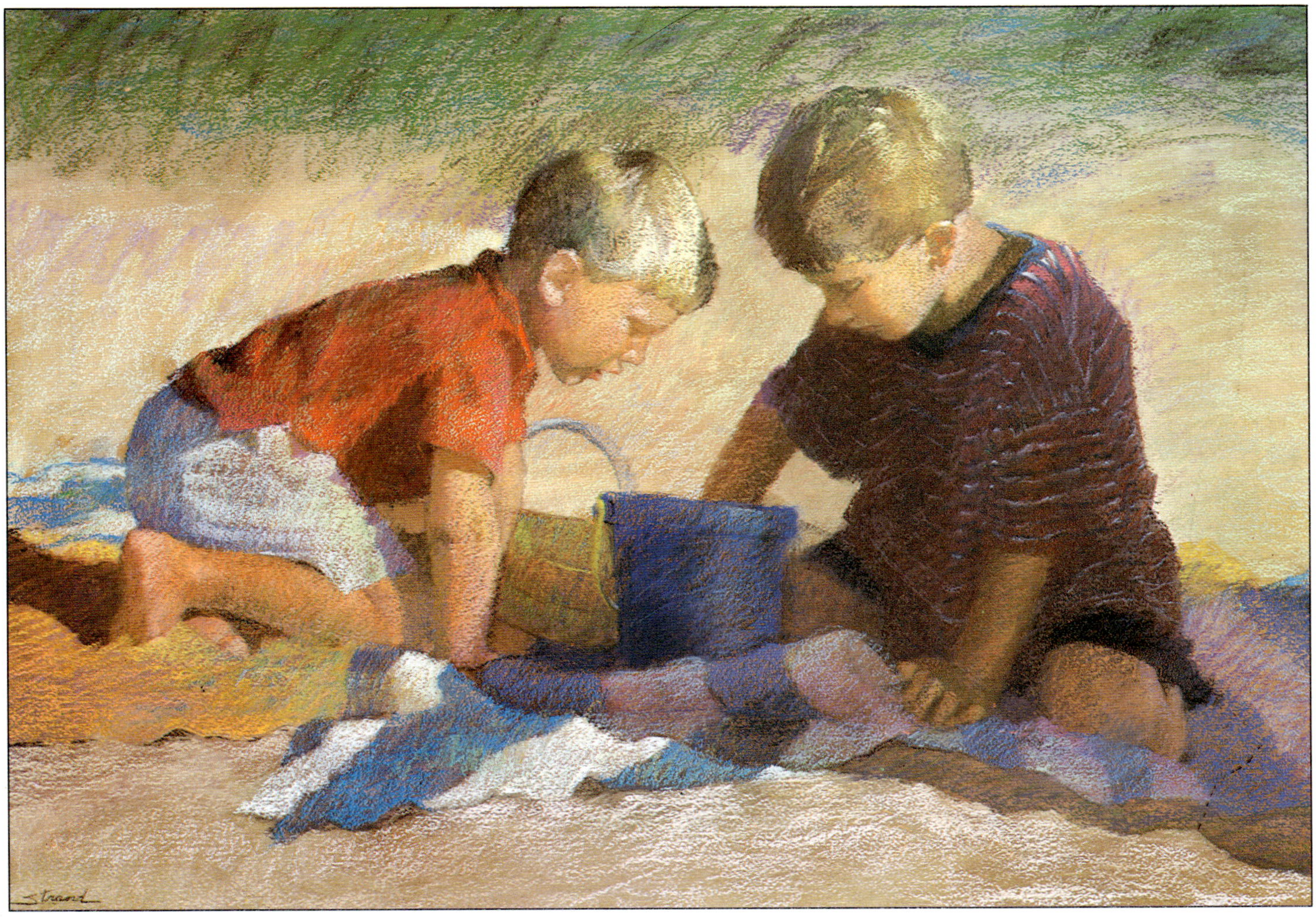

DEMONSTRATION

Ken Paine, a professional portrait painter, works occasionally in oils and acrylics, but principally in pastels, which he loves for their spontaneity and directness. He has a remarkable talent for achieving a likeness with no apparent effort, but his paintings also express character and atmosphere, which he sees as equally, if not more, important. By building up his colours thickly, in a highly painterly technique, he also achieves an almost sculptural feeling of weight and solidity. For this demonstration he has worked on grey Mi-Teintes paper, using the "right" side – that is, the more heavily textured one.

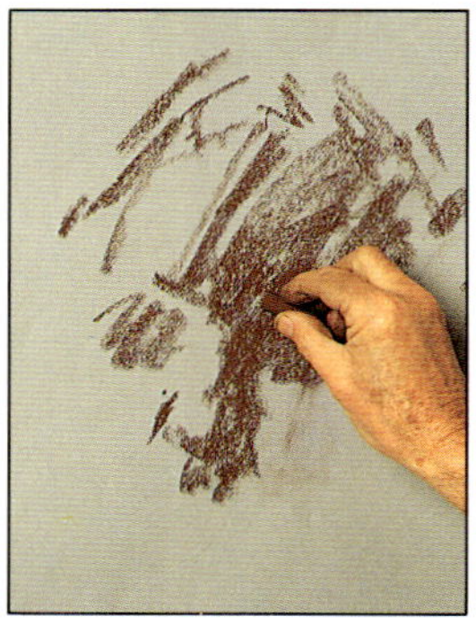

1 The painting is begun in monochrome to provide a basis for the shadowed areas of the skin tones. The marks appear to be almost a random scribble, but already the forms of the face are beginning to emerge.

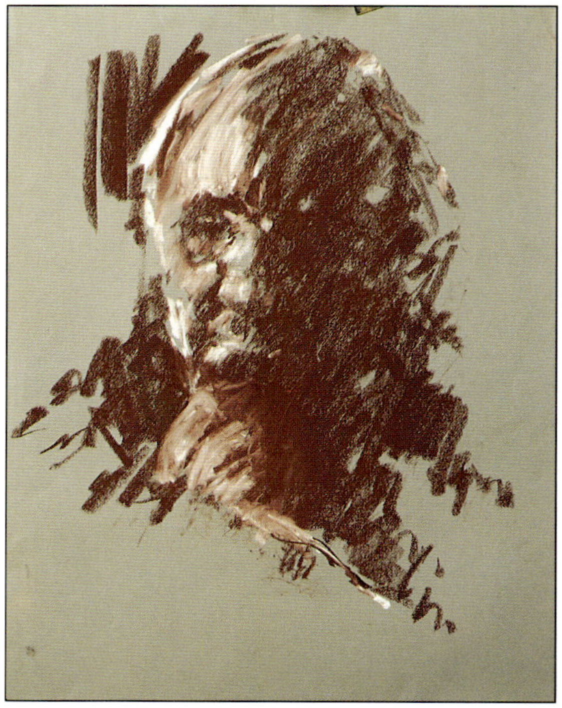

2 The monochrome underpainting, which is now complete, provides a basic tonal structure on which to build up the colours. This method is only suitable for a painting which uses a limited palette of relatively sombre colours – a characteristic of this artist's work.

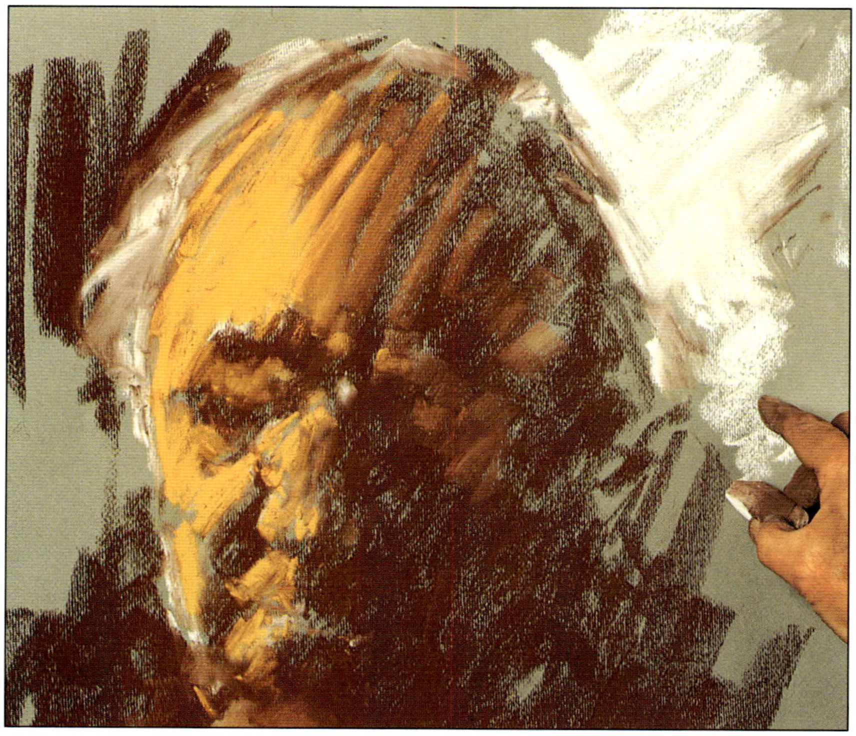

3 The shadowed side of the head will be considerably darkened as the painting progresses, so the artist first lightens the background to enable him to judge the strength of colour needed. Tonal modelling is particularly important, and he continually assesses one tone against another.

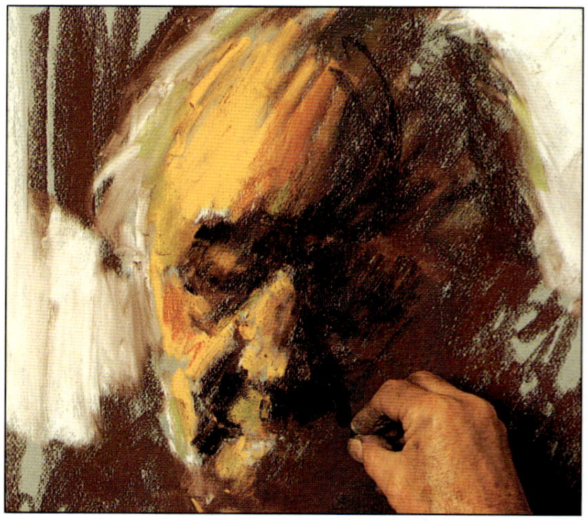

4 Blacks and darker browns are now worked over and into the red-brown underpainting to build up the forms of the head. The artist uses short lengths of thick, soft-pastel sticks, which give the broad strokes he likes and enable him to push the edges of the colours together.

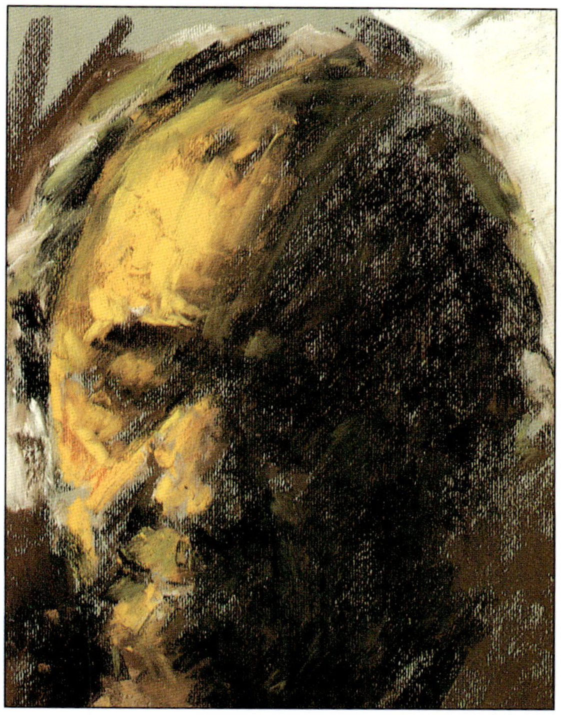

5 With the darker tones established, further work has been done on the lit side of the face. Notice that the pastel is much thicker here; the artist's method is similar to that seen in many oil paintings, where the paint is thickest in the highlight areas, making them stand out from the shadows.

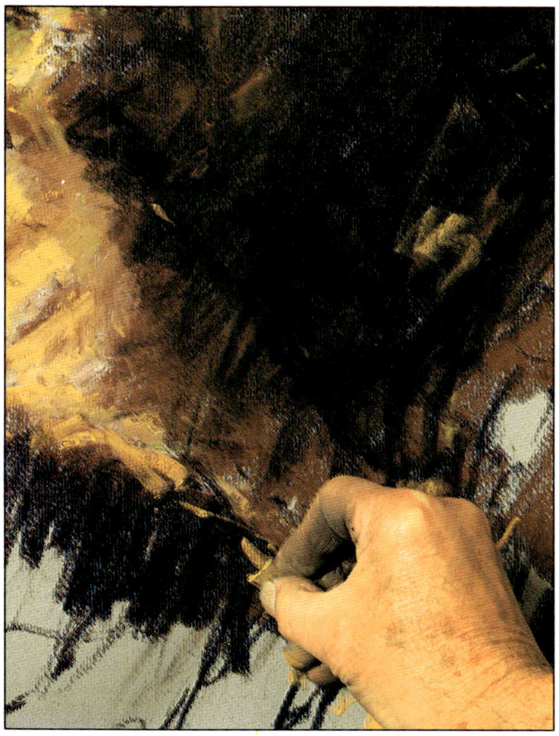

6 The artist had originally planned a hand and wrist as part of the composition (see step 2), and now gives some additional definition to this area. However, he then decided to make a dramatic change, eradicating the hand completely, as you can see in the finished painting.

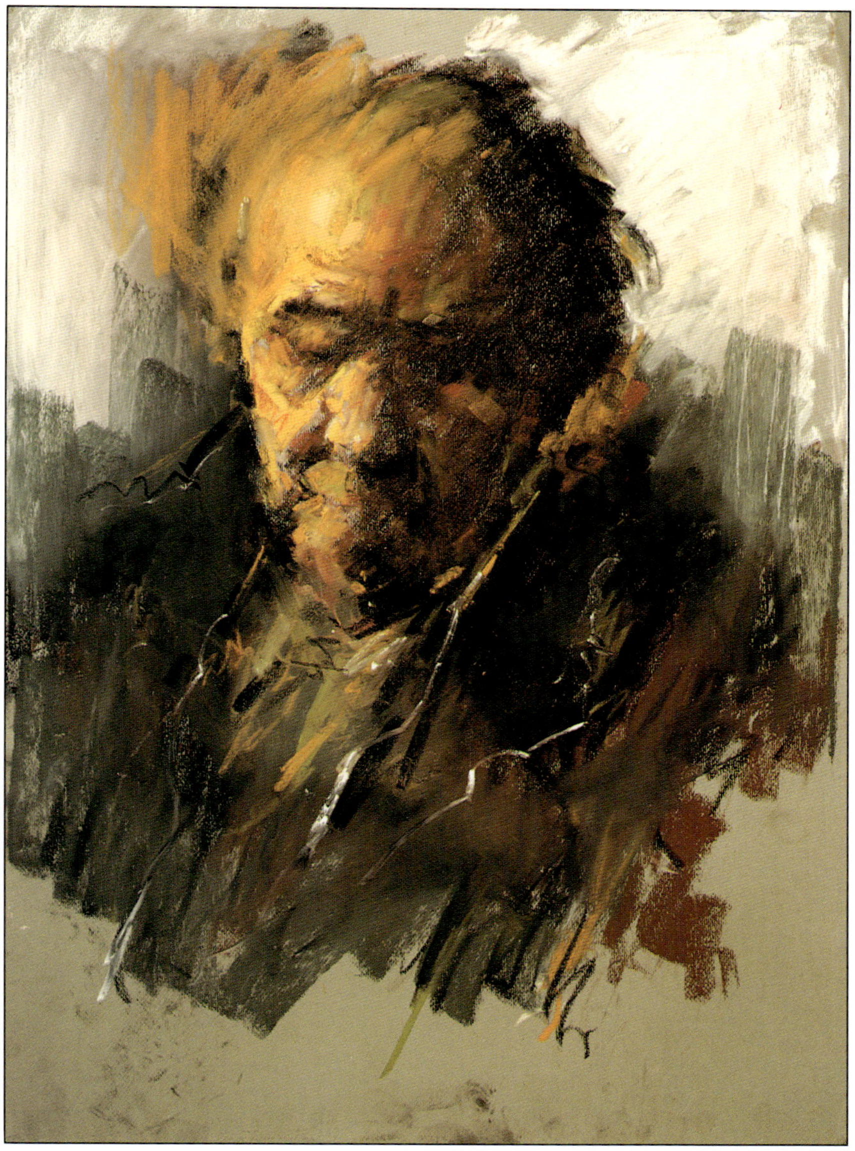

7 A complete transformation has now taken place – the hand has been painted out with heavy applications of dark green and red-brown, and suggestions of detail drawn in with an edge of white pastel (again, notice what fine lines can be produced in this way). The lighter colours below the chin, which suggest a shirt or cravat, balance the head much better than did the hand, and the composition is altogether more satisfactory.

INDEX

PUBLISHER'S ACKNOWLEDGEMENTS

The Author and Publisher would like to thank the following companies for supplying materials used in the making of this book.

Cornelissen & Son Ltd
105 Great Russell Street
London WC1B 3RY

Daler-Rowney Ltd
PO Box 10
Southern Industrial Estate
Bracknell
Berkshire
RG12 8ST

Russell & Chapple Ltd
Canvas & Art Materials
23 Monmouth Street
London WC2H 9DE

Winsor & Newton
Whitefriars Avenue
Wealdstone
Harrow
Middlesex
HA3 5RH